THE HIGHLANDS
OF SCOTLAND
in Pictures

THE PASS OF THE SPANIARDS

In GLEN SHIEL, Wester Ross, the Jacobites, assisted by Spanish troops, were routed in 1719 by the Hanoverians in the battle which was to seal the fate of the Rebellion known to historians as "The Nineteen." The Spaniards' ill-fortune is commemorated in the defile through the mountains of Glen Shiel known to this day as the Pass of the Spaniards.

THE
HIGHLANDS OF
SCOTLAND

in Pictures

By ALASDAIR ALPIN MacGREGOR

WITH A FOREWORD BY
THE RT. HON. THOMAS JOHNSTON, LL.D., F.E.I.S.,
SECRETARY OF STATE FOR SCOTLAND, 1941–5

CONTENTS
*

ODHAMS PRESS LTD.   LONG ACRE, LONDON

EARLY MORNING AT KIRN, DUNOON

DUNOON, situated in the Cowal district of Argyllshire, is one of the most celebrated of the many watering-places on the splendid Firth of Clyde. The introduction of steam navigation in the nineteenth century brought it within easy reach of Glasgow, transforming it, in a few years, from a humble clachan into one of the most prosperous of resorts.

4

Foreword

TAKE a thousand artists or a thousand cameramen and turn them loose on tour through the beautiful Highlands of Scotland. Tell them to go where they will and come back with their choice of the most magnificent, the most inspiring and the most alluring of the myriad vistas and wonders in scenery that they encountered, and you might well get a thousand different selections and choices.

In the following pages Alasdair Alpin MacGregor has provided his selection. I, for my part, would have included in my list such cameos from my memory as that awe-inspiring, never-to-be-forgotten picture of the Red Cuillins seen against the background of a setting sun from the hill above Sligachan, though that cameo might have been barred since its locus is in Skye, and Skye is an island and not therefore in the Highlands proper; and I have engravings on my memory of the Kyles of Bute and of a scene northwards from the Duke's Road above Aberfoyle (perhaps the most popular road in all Scotland nowadays for family motor parties); and there is the picture of Loch Awe between Portsonachan and Portinisherrich (though sometimes it is be-plagued with midges, and you had better have some Tourist Board insect-repellent cream with you when you take that journey); and then there is the glory and majesty of the view on an autumn evening from the Lodge looking westward along Loch Affric towards the Five Sisters of Kintail; and there is the view from the crest of Mam Ratagan above Loch Duich. I have looked north from Darjeeling to the mountain mysteries of Kinchinjunga, and have seen the Canadian Rockies at daybreak, but in awesome splendour they rate with me no higher than does the view from Mam Ratagan. And there are widely travelled connoisseurs of the scenic glories of the world who would give high priority to the picture of the Spey above Craigellachie.

There is a story of an aged Belgian gentleman who was walking along Princes Street, Edinburgh, one evening during the first year of our Festival. Suddenly the old Castle on the rocky height above was floodlit, and there appeared in the heavens an awesome mystery. It was as if some medieval artist, say Albrecht Dürer, had rolled out for us from the darkness of the night sky a segment of a Holy City, and had bathed it in a brilliant light. The old Belgian, it is said, got down on his knees on the pavement and thanked God for the vision that had been granted him.

So also do travellers feel who have journeyed north on the Highland Line, and felt the solace from the beauty and the power of the hills. Around the corner

5

of a glen or over the breast of a mountain top there come vistas of Nature in her greatest glory, and if the traveller be Scots, and particularly if he be of Highland ancestry, there is more than beauty that has laid its hand upon him—there is romance too, history, and a linking-up somehow with his forebears who have long departed.

Alas, there are many areas from which the peasantry has gone; many areas in which parish after parish, glen after glen, are all but deserted, and few now reside amid the surrounding loveliness and the majesty. One through road in Sutherlandshire runs for thirty-four miles, and so far as the eye can see east or west, north or south, there are only six chimneys asmoke, and of the six chimneys three are of shooting lodges occupied only for a brief period every year. The bold kindred have vanished, though their descendants now are spread thickly over the United States and the great Dominions beyond the seas.

The immigration gains to the New World from Highland stock have steadily depleted the old homeland. But vigorous efforts are being put forward to arrest the depopulation, and these efforts, at least in some parishes, are succeeding. The Forestry Commissioners are organizing year after year steadily augmented employments in timber raising, and they estimate that in less than fifty years from now there will actually be more people employed in Scots forest and ancillary services than in Scots coal-mining, and a considerable proportion of that forestry population will be of necessity in the Highland area. The Duke of Westminster, says the London *Times*, has by tree planting "completely arrested the depopulation of the coastal districts in North-west Sutherland." Sir John Stirling-Maxwell, one of the greatest silviculturalists of this century, has raised forests on the wild peat-covered Moor of Rannoch. At Loch Ard thousands of acres of barren slopes are being clothed with a verdant coverage of trees; from the forests of Loch Ard twenty-five years hence there will be an annual timber output of 20,000 tons; already there are a hundred and twenty workers employed, by 1970 that figure will have grown to four hundred. Forest villages spring up. At Dalavich on Loch Awe-side, at Inchnacardoch upon Loch Ness, in Cowal, and in a hundred other once deserted tracts, rural life begins again: a Highland economy is being reborn.

The hydro-electric schemes too, which so many people feared would bring destruction to amenity in the Highlands, have in fact proved the reverse of destructive. At Pitlochry (which was the centre of dispute when the Tummel-Garry scheme was in its initial stages) the Merchants Association have unanimously recorded their thanks for the changes brought by the hydro works and dams, and for the amenities preserved and indeed improved. Hotels which opposed the scheme now issue brochures advertising the enhanced attractions which have made Pitlochry Scotland's number one inland holiday resort. There are new attractions, new amenities, new life and new hope in the Highlands.

ON A ROAD IN MORAR

THE Morar district of Inverness-shire, with its soft climate and its sheen-white sands, is one of the loveliest and most romantic in Britain. It lies, as it were, at the end of the popular Road to the Isles. From Mallaig, where road and rail terminate, many of the Inner Hebrides, including Skye, are but a few miles away. Morar's sheep-haunted pastures, its strands and seascapes have attracted artists from all parts of the world.

7

THE HIGHLANDS OF SCOTLAND

ORKNEY ISLANDS

Cape Wrath

Pentland Firth

Dunnet Head
Duncansby Head

Thurso
R.Thurso
WICK
CAITHNESS
Lybster

Foinaven 2980
Ben Hope 3040
R.Naver
R.Halladale

Ben Hee 2864

SUTHERLAND

Lochinver
Suilven 2399
Ben More 3273
Loch Shin
Helmsdale

The Minch

R.Oykell

Loch Ewe
Ullapool
Dunrobin Castle
DORNOCH

NORTH SEA

Loch Torridon
Loch Maree
Ben Dearg 3547
Ben Wyvis 3429
Tain
Moray Firth
ELGIN

ROSS & CROMARTY

Slioch 3217
DINGWALL
Cromarty Firth
Cromarty
NAIRN
Forres
Fochabers

TORRIDON
Beauly
INVERNESS
Culloden Moor
MORAY
R.Deveron

Applecross
NORTH WESTERN
NAIRN

SKYE
Mam Soul 3862
L.Duich
Ben Attow 3383
Loch Ness
R.Nairn
R.Findhorn
Grantown
R.Don

R.Spey

L.Hourn
L.Nevis
L.Oich
MONADHLIATH MTS.
Rothiemurchus
Cairn Gorm 4084
CAIRNGORM MTS

Mallaig
Arisaig
L.Morar
L.Arkaig
INVERNESS
Kingussie
R.Dee

Glenfinnan
L.Lochy
L.Laggan

L.Shiel
Fort William
Ben Nevis 4406
L.Ericht
Ben-y-Glae 3671
R.North Esk

ARDNAMURCHAN
ARDGOUR
Blair Atholl
R.South Esk

Loch Sunart
GlenCoe
GRAMPIAN MOUNTAINS

MULL
Loch Linnhe
APPIN
Glen Etive
Schiehallion 3547
PERTH
Dunkeld

Loch Etive
Ben Lawers 3984
Loch Tay
R.Tay

Oban
Kilchurn Castle
Ben Lui 3708
Killin
R.Almond

Ben More 3843
L.Earn
Crieff
PERTH
Tarbert

ARGYLL
INVERARAY
Loch Katrine
R.Earn

L.Awe
The Cobbler 2891
TROSSACHS
Boune
OCHIL HILLS
GIGHA

JURA
L.Long
Loch Lomond
R.Teith
ARRAN

Lochgilphead
Loch Fyne
R.Forth
KINTYRE
Kilbrennan Sound

Sound of Jura
Dunoon
Saddell

Tarbert
DAVAAR
Campbeltown

Mull of Kintyre

Scale of Miles
0   10   20   30   40   50

Between April, 1948, and December, 1951, the Hydro-Electric Board in the North of Scotland has connected up seventy thousand new consumers, almost three-quarters of them being in rural and remote areas.

For a variety of reasons, notable among them long-distance transport, the installation of large industries in the Highlands is a matter of considerable difficulty. Many people indeed would regard the planting of a large-scale industry in the Highlands as wholly undesirable and likely still further to accentuate emigration from the remoter areas. What at any rate is more immediately possible and desirable is encouragement of small-scale industries stemming naturally from local conditions, and scattered here and there over the Highland counties.

The Hydro-Electric Board is rather proceeding along the lines of making successful experiments in the resuscitation, for example, of the stone-quarrying industry; some saw-milling and wood-working industries will develop through the operations of the Forestry Commissioners and the Highland Panel and the Herring Industry Board, and such enterprising lairds as Lord Lovat in Strathglass and Mr. Hobbs at Inverlochy, and the Ben Challum Estate in Perthshire, with their more-cattle-on-the-hills projects, all give promise of employment indigenous to Highland traditions and customs. Nor are we without hope that this generation will discover effective and economic means of disposal of great blankets of peat which cover wide areas in the north. Under these great peat deposits it is known that there is land with considerable agricultural possibilities, as was shown when parts of Flanders Moss in Stirlingshire were washed away to the Firth of Forth by Lord Kames more than a century and a half ago.

Despite, too, some foolish restrictions placed upon our seasonal hotels in the Highlands by a universal application of wholly unsuitable and inappropriate regulations under the Catering Act, the Highland tourist trade grows. It grows in spite of these restrictions, and when they are removed (as they must be) it is the confident belief of the Scottish Tourist Board that the scenery, the history, the remoteness, the pipe music of Caledonia will make it one of the most attractive tourist areas in all the world. Already, measured in terms of employment, it is our sixth largest Scottish industry. It has all-the-year-round fog-free areas. There are places with sunshine records comparable with the Isle of Wight; the annual rainfall on the Moray Firth is as low as the annual rainfall in London; the Shetlands have two hours per day more light in summer than has Cornwall; we have unparalleled angling resources; we are the motherland for some twenty million men and women of Scots ancestry overseas.

FINTRY,
STIRLINGSHIRE.

Thomas Johnston

FISHING-CRAFT AT TARBERT, LOCH FYNE

ON THE isthmus between East and West Lochs Tarbert, separating the Argyllshire districts of Knapdale and Kintyre, is the thriving village of Tarbert, after which the words Loch Fyne are usually added to distinguish it readily from the other Tarberts of Scotland. It is famed for the Loch Fyne herrings landed from the small fishing-boats actually built there.

The Western Highlands

BY THE Western Highlands one usually means those parts of Celtic Scotland embracing the vast mainland of Argyll and all the western seaboard of Inverness-shire. This comprises territory as far south as the Mull of Kintyre, and as far north as Inverness-shire's boundary with Wester Ross. Any such demarcation, of course, must be a little arbitrary. However, for most purposes, and certainly for our present, it appears to be the most practicable. This is the region of the Highlands which, for more than one reason, is the best known. Much of it is traversed either by the railway which, at Oban, reaches its terminus within a few yards of the tides of western Argyll, or by that which, at Mallaig, does likewise, at no greater distance from the seas of western Inverness-shire, within easy reach of the Small Isles and of the Isle of Skye. Both routes run through stretches of Highland territory certainly unrivalled for scenic beauty and for romantic association. Mountains and tumbled rocks lie on every side by whichever route one goes.

Though Argyll is by no means without inland lochs of great beauty, such as Loch Awe, its glory resides in the *sea*-lochs selvedged by mountains. This is due largely to a configuration which has bequeathed to the county a coastline of enormous length. For beauty of physical form, as well as for the delicate subtleties of colour, there is nothing to compare with the Firth of Lorne, or with such tidal lochs as Loch Etive and Loch Fyne, Loch Linnhe and Loch Leven. Many of these are overshadowed by the mighty Grampians. Ben Nevis, loftiest of Britain's peaks, casts its shadow upon much of Loch Linnhe, for example. The mountains, between which lies Glen Coe, are reflected in Loch Leven.

The route to Mallaig is perhaps the more beautiful. Here is a countryside which, until the opening of the West Highland Railway toward the close of last century, was scarcely known to the outside world. True, the road led one northward by the Bonnie, Bonnie Banks into the wilds of Argyll, and eventually across the sombre Moor of Rannoch and down Glen Coe to the western tides; but the journeying was arduous, and tended to become more and more so as one approached Fort William, the original terminus of the railway just mentioned. Beyond Fort William the difficulties of inland travel increased, since the road by Glenfinnan and Morar—"by Ailort and by Morar to the sea," as Dr. Kenneth MacLeod sings in "The Road to the Isles"—remained so primitive that nothing on wheels, except a slow, jolting, lumbering cart, could tackle it. The West

Highland Railway—that splendid engineering accomplishment—then brought this supremely beautiful land within a few hours' reach of Glasgow.

Today road and railway convey an ever-increasing number of travellers right into the heart of the Western Highlands. Not even their well-earned reputation for humidity deters! West Highland rain, people say, is different from rain elsewhere. And why? Surely the answer is that it lends to the scene that misty half-light effect which stirs the poetic imagination! It also explains, of course, those unbelievable blues and greens and purples which, year after year, draw artists as far afield as Morar, and into the remote corners of Clan Ranald's Moidart.

Of history and romance there is no dearth in this countryside. The Massacre of Glen Coe, which occurred as long ago as 1692, still grips one. At the scene of the tragedy one halts for a moment, even when speeding through this magnificent glen, encouraged by the fine surface of its New Road. At Ballachulish House, not far off, Major Duncanson wrote to Captain Robert Campbell of Glenlyon his infamous letter beginning with the well-known words: "You are hereby ordered to fall upon the Rebells, the M'Donalds of Glenco, and putt all to the Sword under Seventy. You are to have a special care that the old Fox and his sons doe upon no account escape your hands."

If one were to look for another outstanding incident in West Highland history, one would find it readily in Appin, just round the corner from Glen Coe, as it were. There, in 1752, Colin Campbell of Glenure, commonly known as the Red Fox, and factor for certain forfeited Highland estates at the time of the Great Rebellion, was shot dead while proceeding on horseback by the Lettermore. Who fired the shot remains one of Britain's historical mysteries. But the man who, the following year, paid the penalty for it, on the gallows overlooking the ferry at Ballachulish, is known to history as James of the Glen. He was James Stewart, who tenanted the small farm of Acharn, in Duror of Appin. He had been found guilty, according to the rules of justice of the day, of complicity in the crime his kinsman, Allan Breac Stewart, was *said* to have committed.

One other historical figure's association with the Western Highlands must be mentioned—another Stewart—Prince Charles Edward. Here, at Loch nan Uamh, he landed in his endeavour to wrest from the Hanoverians the kingdom of his fathers. Here, at Glenfinnan, at the spot by the head of Loch Shiel where stands his monument, he raised the Jacobite Standard on behalf of his father, the Old Chevalier, Great Britain's lawful King. Here he embarked for France, with Locheil and several others who had taken part in his ill-fated enterprise, "leaving us all in a worse case than he found us," as a contemporary Jacobite tells. His hopes had vanished at Culloden. So evergreen in this countryside is the memory of Bonnie Prince Charlie that one meets natives who speak of him as though he had passed through it but yesterday.

MOUNTAINEERING ON BEN NEVIS

BEN NEVIS is the loftiest of Britain's mountains. Its summit, at 4,406 feet, is a hundred feet higher than that of Ben MacDhui, in the Cairngorms. Mountaineering, both in summer and in snow-time, has always been popular upon it, especially among those whose delight it is to traverse the more perilous routes to its summit, in preference to the less arduous, one of which is in no way strenuous. This picture shows the crater-shaped corrie of Sgurr a' Mhaim from Sgurr a' Mhuic, with the depths of Glen Nevis between them.

13

THE ROAD TO INVERARAY

OF ALL the roads through the Highlands along which one is attracted with the camera in winter, that to Inveraray—Neil Munro's birth-place, and his Half Town of the Lost Pibroch— is the most alluring. By the time one has reached the shores of Loch Long and can look across to the entrance to Glen Croe (*below*), with the snow-bound Cobbler towering nearly 3,000 feet above it, one is well on the way toward the most fascinating of Scotland's *little* towns. The traverses whereby General Wade carried his military road up Glen Croe (*right*) to Rest-and-be-Thankful still constitute a formidable route, even in summer. This was seen when, in 1921, the massive bells for All Saints', at Inveraray, came this way from Loughborough. The steep acclivities and hairpin bends of "The Rest" proved so great an obstacle that the three largest of them had to lie by the roadside for a night or two until more powerful tractors could be brought to the scene. The natives thought they were giant beehives which the Duke of Argyll had ordered for the gardens of his castle

at Inveraray. It was, indeed, a triumph when, at last, St. Molaise's two tons and more of solid metal reached the summit of this famous Highland pass. Never before had anything quite so ponderous been transported through such difficult West Highland territory. The Bells of Inveraray now hang in the belfry tower at All Saints' Church. General Wade's road over "The Rest" was built immediately after the 1715 Rebellion. A stone seat, inscribed "Rest-and-be-Thankful," was erected at its highest point to replace a simpler one erected there by its builders, and alluded to by Wordsworth in the lines:

> *Doubling and doubling with laborious walk,*
> *Who, that has gained at length the*
> *wished-for height,*
> *This brief this simple wayside call*
> *can slight,*
> *And rest not thankful?*

It was the poet's sister, Dorothy, who referred to this stretch of the road to Inveraray as having insinuated itself into the very mountains.

15

TOWNS AND VILLAGES OF ARGYLL

CAMPBELTOWN (*top, left*), with a population of roughly eight thousand, is a thriving community situated at the head of the loch of the same name, toward the southern extremity of the Kintyre peninsula. It was given its present name in 1700 as a compliment to the Duke of Argyll. Its excellent harbour is protected by Davaar, the island at the mouth of the loch, connected with the mainland at low water by the long, narrow strip of land known as the Dorlin. Herring-fishing used to be the town's chief industry. Its inhabitants have also been interested in net-making, rope-making, shipbuilding, and whisky-distilling. At Campbeltown coal has been shipped at various times from the neighbouring mine at Drumlemble. The town, besides having its own steamer service, is visited twice daily by a plane flown from Renfrew, Glasgow's airport. The little town of Inveraray (*bottom, left*), on Loch Fyne, needs no introduction to readers of Neil Munro's *John Splendid*, nor to students of the murder, in 1752, of Colin Campbell of Glenure, factor for the forfeited estates of Mamore and Ardsheal. At the north end of the town are the Old County Buildings, an apartment of which was the court-room where the historic trial of James of the Glen took place. James was accused before a Campbell jury of having been accessory. These buildings, so intimately associated with his fate—he was found guilty—are now the Argyll Estate Offices. Not far from the town is Inveraray Castle, seat of the Duke of Argyll, built by the third duke about the middle of the eighteenth century, and standing on the right bank of the River Aray. Behind it rises Dun Cuach, the densely wooded hill seen in the background of the picture. In ancient days it was a watch-tower. Certain isles in the Firth of Lorne are known appropriately as the Slate Islands because of their nature, the principal isles being Seil, Easdale, and Luing. In each of these, slate-quarrying has been the inhabitants' mainstay for at least two centuries. The quarrymen and their families live in rows or clusters of small, whitewashed cottages, such as one sees in the picture (*above*) showing Seil from Easdale. Quarrying began at the latter as long ago as 1631.

17

HIGH SUMMER IN ARGYLL

AT ONE time both Glen Strae (*above*) and Loch Awe (*right*) formed a part of the extensive patrimony of the MacGregors, a clan as famed in song and story for its misfortunes as for its royal lineage and for the intrepidity of its leading men. Today this countryside knows little of the wild Clan Gregor. Centuries of persecution and proscription reduced it to impotence, except in the realm of history and romance. The corridors of Kilchurn Castle, its stronghold on an islet at the Strath of Orchy end of Loch Awe, one of the largest and most important freshwater lochs in Scotland, are silent and decayed. Tradition tells how the MacGregors were ousted from Kilchurn by the wily Campbells. Pennant relates that in 1745 Campbell of Breadalbain repaired the castle's great tower, and garrisoned the place "for the service of the Government in order to prevent the rebels [the Jacobites] from making use of that great pass across the kingdom, but is now a ruin, having been lately struck by lightning." Not far from Loch Awe and Kilchurn is Glen Strae, with its poignant memories of the hapless MacGregors. The chief of that branch of the clan, in giving asylum to a member of the Clan Lamont who he knew had just slain his son and heir, provided Sir Walter Scott with the theme of *The Lady of the Lake*.

HIGHLANDERS AT WORK

SPARSELY populated though the Highlands are, the industries and occupations of the inhabitants are many and varied. Large-scale agriculture is possible only where fertility will allow, such as in Easter Ross and parts of Perthshire. Yet the struggle to wrest a livelihood from the land has gone on, unceasingly, for centuries, and often with little to show for much earnest application. The fertile patches between the mountains, however, are zealously husbanded. Not the least important harvest is that which provides winter feeding for livestock in territory notoriously poor in pasture during the winter months. Thus attention must be given to the hay crop, in the gathering of which everyone co-operates, as at Pole Farm, in the Lochgoilhead district of Argyll (*opposite, top*). Fishing has always been a complementary means of livelihood in the maritime parts of the Highlands, though the fishing industry has declined much in recent decades. For all that, the crofter-fisherman, owning his own boat (*opposite, bottom right*), manages to derive from land and sea a living which, though none too sufficing, affords him just that measure of independence of which he was once so proud. The income lost in recent years by the decline of the herring fishings, as indeed also of the line fishings (the latter being attributed largely to the destruction of the spawning-beds by trawlers operating within the prohibited areas), has been recovered to some extent by the lobster-fishings. Improvements in sea, road, rail, and air transport have made it possible to dispatch the lobsters to the great centres of population with a minimum of delay, and at prices encouraging to those who, among the Highland sea-lochs and skerries, pursue this calling. Salmon net fishing is also carried on remuneratively, especially where conducted by fishers operating in such waters as Loch Feochan (*below*), a sea-loch near Oban. Many handicrafts survive, though on a small scale. The spinning-wheel maker, for example, is still with us. Most of the spinning-wheels made by Donald Sinclair of Loch Awe-side (*opposite, bottom left*) are exported.

OBAN (*above*, as seen from the Pulpit Hill) is pleasantly situated at the head of a small and almost landlocked bay. It faces the green Isle of Kerrera, which affords its spacious harbour shelter in all weathers. In addition to its being a railway terminus reached direct from London, it provides an almost bewildering variety of transport to scenes of beauty and romance. The number of steamer and motor-coach excursions from it far exceeds that available in any other town of its size. From it one reaches with the greatest of ease several of the Inner Hebrides, including Mull and Iona. To the application of steam to navigation the town owes its development from the few thatched fishermen's cottages which comprised it at the close of the eighteenth century. Round the "tolerable inn" visited by Johnson and Boswell in 1773 the number of dwellings began to increase, so

22

that by the time Sir Walter Scott arrived there in 1814 its population had risen to six hundred. The enterprising pioneers in steamboat transport in the Western Highlands and Islands gave the place its first major fillip. Oban Bay is a place of constant activity. In addition to the Hebridean steamers sailing from it and arriving at it daily, it is a favourite resort of yachts, since the town is the headquarters of the Royal Highland Yacht Club, founded in 1881, the members of which fly the blue ensign of the Navy and a blue badge bearing a crown on a St. Andrew's Cross. Ships of Her Majesty's Navy also frequent the bay. Add to all this activity that created by the herring drifters (*above*) now landing their catches at its harbour, and one sees how busy and important a centre this lovely West Highland town has become. Oban, as is well known, is inclined to be somewhat rainy.

ARGYLL is rich in ancient castles. Some of these are in ruins: others are still occupied. An excellent example of the latter is to be seen in Barcaldine Castle (*left*), standing amid beautiful scenery not far from the shore of Loch Creran, and but two miles to the north of the site of Beregonium, which Ptolemy mentions, and which is believed to have been the seat of the Fingalian kings, of the legends and traditions concerning whom this countryside is so full. Barcaldine Castle, the ancient seat of the Campbells of Barcaldine, was built in the fifteenth century by Sir Duncan Campbell of Lochow. It remained in Campbell hands until 1842. Fifty-four years later it was bought back by the tenth Laird of Barcaldine, who restored it and rendered it habitable once more. By the shore of Loch Fyne, not far from Inveraray, is Dundarave (*below*), the old castle of the MacNachtan chiefs. Like Barcaldine, it lay in ruins for many years. Not until the present century was it restored as a habitable place. Its restoration was carried out by the late Sir

Robert Lorimer. The additions necessary for its adaptation to modern requirements conform strictly to the original Scots baronial keep. In the days of the MacNachtans the ancient keep was reputed to be one of the most hospitable in the Scottish Highlands. Perched on a promontory on the northern outskirts of Oban are the ruins of Dunollie Castle (*right*), supposed to have been built in the twelfth century. In olden days it was the seat of the MacDougalls of Lorne, and is still the property of their descendant, MacDougall of MacDougall, Chief of the Clan MacDougall, whose modern mansion lies in its shadow. Preserved in the latter is that celebrated heirloom, the Brooch of Lorne, which MacDougall took from Robert the Bruce in their encounter at Dalrigh in 1306. Little is known of the early history of Tarbert Castle (*below*), said to have been built by Robert the Bruce. Its site, overlooking a great stretch of Loch Fyne and the hills beyond, is one of the most imposing in the Western Highlands. Today the castle is a mere shell.

ONE of the least frequented of Highland valleys is Glen Etive, for the road passing sinuously along its base leads nowhere but to the head of the lovely loch of the same name. The upper reaches of the glen are dominated by those graceful peaks, the Buachaille Etive Mor and the Buachaille Etive Beag, popularly known as the Shepherds of Etive. They form part of the Royal Forest of Etive. Halfway down the glen is Dalness, the estate

F THE SHEPHERDS OF ETIVE

purchased in 1937 by the National Trust for Scotland, affording mountaineers and rock-climbers, for their respective purposes, some of the finest territory in Britain. Glen Etive is dear to the Gael because of its close association with Deirdre of the Sorrows and with the Sons of Uisneach. The site of Deirdre's home is still pointed out by Celtic storytellers who recite the tragedy which befell her—one of Three True Sorrows of Storytelling.

THE HAUNTED HOUSE

STANDING pleasantly in its own policies not far from the point at which the River Awe reaches Loch Etive is the fine mansion known as Inverawe House, the oldest part of which dates from the sixteenth century. This house is famous because of its association with one of the most carefully documented of all ghost stories. Briefly stated, Duncan Campbell of Inverawe was visited thrice by the apparition of a slain kinsman. The apparition urged him not to shelter any longer at Inverawe House the murderer, and uttered, as a warning, a strange, unheard of word—*Ticonderoga!* Shortly afterwards Duncan, while serving with the Black Watch, died of wounds in America, following upon an attack on the French fort at Carillon, a place known to the Red Indians as Ticonderoga! At the moment of his death, two relatives of his, a father and son, were asleep in the same room, but in different beds, in Inverawe House, when the son woke to observe a phantom in Highland uniform stooping over his father's

bed. The father, when told of this in the morning, expressed no surprise, but explained to his son that he had seen the ghost of their kinsman, Duncan Campbell of Inverawe, who had just lost his life as the result of a great battle in America, at a place called Ticonderoga! When the Gazette reached Britain several weeks later, it confirmed Duncan's death, on that very day, at Ticonderoga! He fell while assailing its fortifications.

OLD POST OFFICE AT GUALACHAN

SPARSELY peopled though Glen Etive is, one finds at Gualachan, where a mountain stream hastens to enter Loch Etive, the old post office (*left*) serving this remote countryside. In summer this lovely glen is seen by many, since it is traversed by motor-coaches which meet the little steamer sailing daily up Loch Etive. In 1937 that part of Glen Etive known anciently as the Royal Forest of Dalness, comprising thirteen thousand acres of sheep-grazing and ten thousand of deer-forest, became the property of the National Trust for Scotland. The previous year members of the Scottish Mountaineering Club had approached the Trust to ascertain whether it would accept this property, provided a considerable proportion of the purchase price were met by its members. It was acquired through the efforts of the Pilgrim Trust, the Scottish Mountaineering Club, and kindred organizations.

A WEST HIGHLAND VILLAGE AND SOME LOCAL INHABITANTS

IN VILLAGES such as that of Glencoe (seen *above*, with the mists deploying among the mountains at sundown in autumn), one may encounter the whole gamut of Highland rural society. The tinkers often come this way with their caravans, pitching their bivouacs at recognized spots for a few days, and tethering or hobbling their ponies upon wayside pastures often more luscious than are the adjacent meadow-lands. The tinkers' arrival in the neighbourhood is frequently heard before it is witnessed, since at least one male member of each contingent (*top left, opposite*) carries his bagpipes everywhere with him, heralding the clan's coming with a skirl or two, and frequenting thereafter the precincts of any public-house in the locality, to play lustily for the charitable coppers which accumulate until he is able to afford as stiff a dram as anybody. In villages like this, moreover, one finds aged Highlanders living quietly in retirement. Some of them may be widows of great age, such as we see in the case of the Glencoe nonagenarian seated outside her cottage. Others may be retired soldiers or sailors or, perhaps, stalkers, like Lachlan MacKenzie, the representative of the fraternity seen on the opposite page, with his homespun jacket and his tall stalking-stick. Highland villages are famed for their nonagenarian and centenarian residents. It would seem as though life in these parts, so free from bustle and mental anxiety, is conducive to longevity. In this connection one is reminded of the classical case of Mary MacCrain, who lived, they say, to a hundred and twenty-four, and whose father is recorded as having spent a hundred and eighty Christmasses in his own house! The fourth photograph on the page opposite is that of a typical crofter-woman of North Ballachulish.

GLEN COE AND BEN NEVIS

ONE of the outstanding achievements in road-making in Britain during the nineteen-twenties was the reconstruction of the Glasgow–Glen Coe–Fort William Road, which now traverses a section of the desolate Moor of Rannoch hitherto unapproachable so far as vehicular traffic was concerned. The New Road, as it is called, in order to differentiate it from the Old, makes for Glen Coe not by Inveroran and the Black Mount, but by the southern shore of Loch Tulla, passing within shouting range of the sheep-farm and ruined castle of Achallader, before it strikes across the Moor of Rannoch at some distance to the east of the Old. It by-passes the historic Kingshouse Inn to descend Glen Coe in fine, even gradients, absorbing here and there, in the glen itself, stretches of the Old Road. In Glen Coe, much of the Old, now lying derelict, can be seen from the New (*left*), since the narrowness of the glen has not permitted of any major divergence. The Old Road provided many a traveller with literary material. One who, in 1800, reached "that most desolate of all human habitations, King's House," believed it to have been "surrounded by an uninhabited desert to the extent of thirty miles, and, with the exception of a miserable patch of garden, there is no attempt at cultivation within reach of human sight." On a wet day, forty-one years later, Charles Dickens journeyed through the Pass of Glen Coe, the scenery of which he described as "perfectly terrible." Westward from Fort William proceeds the Road to the Isles. At Corpach (*above*) one is afforded an excellent view of Ben Nevis, across Loch Linnhe.

A QUIET VILLAGE IN APPIN

APPIN is the name of that mountainous district of Argyll lying roughly between Loch Leven and Loch Creran. The district of Benderloch bounds it on the south-east, while the more inland waters of Loch Linnhe lave it on the north-west. It is a region of quiet beauty. Its shore-lands are among the loveliest in the Highlands. Its villages, all of which lie fairly close to its seaboard, are composed of neat, stone cottages, such as we see in the picture below. Seen in autumn, when phloxes and tropaeolum deck the cottage gardens and doorways, and deciduous foliage is turning scarlet and orange, it is unimaginably beautiful. Many little glens penetrate inland from Appin's seaboard. The best known of these is Glen Duror, and for reasons with which everyone familiar with Highland history and with Stevenson's *Kidnapped* will recall. This lovely land, once the patrimony of the Stewarts of Appin, certainly had its sorrows in the grim period following upon the defeat of Prince Charlie's forces at Culloden. Its inhabitants' loyalty to the Jacobite cause never wavered. It precipitated for them the tragic episode on the Lettermore track related on later pages.

THE PORT APPIN FERRY

WITHIN half a mile of Appin is the north-east end of Lismore, an island with which, throughout the centuries, it has had the closest associations. Between Port Appin and and the jetty situated a little beyond Port Ramsay, in Lismore, plies a ferryboat (*above*, with *King George V* in the background, on one of her summer cruises between Oban and Fort William), enabling the island's two hundred inhabitants to reach or return from the mainland of Argyll almost at any hour, and almost in any weather. Any steamer on the daily service from Oban to Fort William will stop and pick up passengers from the Port Appin–Lismore ferryboat if a flag be waved as the steamer approaches. Alternatively, in answer to blasts from the steamer's siren, the ferry will collect passengers from the steamer.

A HISTORIC MURDER

IN 1752, when James Stewart, or James of the Glen, as he is known to history and romance, was living with his family in the cottage (*left*) now used as part of the steading belonging to the little farm of Acharn, in Duror of Appin, news was brought to him that Colin Campbell of Glenure, factor for certain forfeited Jacobite estates in the neighbourhood, and commonly spoken of as the Red Fox, had been shot dead by *someone* while passing on horseback along the Lettermore hill-track, and at the spot ever since marked by a rude cairn (*right*). James of the Glen was arrested, charged with being guilty, and duly hanged on the Gallows Hill overlooking the ferry at Ballachulish, no distance away. In 1911 the Stewart Society raised on the site of the gallows a memorial to James, "executed on this spot,

8 Nov., 1752, for a crime of which he was not guilty."
The lifeless body of Colin Campbell was borne to
his home, Glenure House (*left*); and a floor-board
in the apartment in which it was laid bears to this
day a bloodstain carefully preserved. It was recently
pointed out to a friend of the author's as the exact
spot where it lay. In the wall of the old, roofless
kirk at Keil, in Appin, is a small bronze tablet
(*right*) marking the spot whereunder the bones of
the unfortunate James of the Glen were ultimately
interred. To this day the question is asked: *Who
killed Colin Campbell, the Red Fox?* This affair has
provided us with one of the most romantic and
intriguing of British historical mysteries.

THE SLATE VILLAGE OF BALLACHULISH

BALLACHULISH village, literally "township of the narrows," extends for a considerable distance, in straggling fashion, along the south shore of Loch Leven, in western Argyll, and on either side of the River Laroch, up to the mouth of Glen Coe. Nearby is the famous passenger and vehicular ferry of the same name, plying where the width of the Loch is but a furlong, and thus saving the traveller toward Fort William the circuitous miles by way of Kinlochleven. The villagers are employed for the most part in slate-quarrying, an industry which has been going on in this neighbourhood since the middle of the eighteenth century. Ballachulish figures much in Highland annals. In Ballachulish House, on 2 February, 1692, Major Duncanson wrote to Robert Campbell of Glen Lyon those fateful words which found expression later in the massacre of the MacDonalds in Glen Coe, nearby.

HIGHLAND GAMES AT TAYNUILT

HIGHLAND Games have long been an integral feature of Highland social life. In Argyll, as elsewhere throughout Celtic Scotland, they are supported with feverish enthusiasm. Almost every community of any size strives, year after year, to celebrate its own, vying with neighbouring communities in such contests as horse-jumping, piping, Highland dancing, running, jumping, hurdles, and tossing the caber—throwing a long and heavy beam or tree-trunk. These games are also the occasion for the competitive display of livestock and of garden and dairy produce. Farmers or their employees parade, for inspection, their best horses, their brightest harnesses, their showiest cattle. Women enter their poultry, as well as such evidence of their industry and handiwork as cheeses, scones, oatcakes and home-spuns. The cottagers bring their best blooms and vegetables. In recent years the ubiquity of the motor-car has greatly added to the popularity of Highland Games, as may be gathered from this picture taken at Taynuilt, where the games were founded in 1859.

CLAN RANALD'S COUNTRY

On St. Finnan's Isle, the Green Isle of Loch Shiel, in Clan Ranald's Country of Moidart, stand the roofless ruins of an ancient chapel surrounded by an ancient burial-place still used by the people of Moidart. On the altar of the chapel (*left*) rests St. Finnan's Bell, with a loose chain attached to it. This bell shared with other Celtic bells a reputation for being endowed with magical powers, such as that of returning of its own accord to its rightful place on the altar when wrongfully removed. On Eilean Tioram, a tidal islet of rock and grass lying a little offshore at the mouth of Loch Moidart, are the noble ruins of Castle Tioram (*below*), Clan Ranald's stronghold in Moidart. On one occasion, when the Great Clan Ranald of the Isles Himself, as he was called, fell out with the government, the Earl of Argyll seized it, but Clan Ranald rallied his henchmen, and retook it. In 1715 the Chief of Clan Ranald directed that the Castle should be set on fire, to prevent its falling into the hands of the Hanoverians.

SHEEP-SHEARING AT ACHALLADER

UNTIL the New Glen Coe Road was built, no sheep-farm in the Highlands lay more remotely than did Achallader, in Glen Orchy, the farmhouse itself and the steading appurtenant thereto nestling at the foot of that mighty mass of the Grampians known as Ben Achallader. This picture shows the late Duncan Smith and his men at shearing operations (note the white fleeces in the foreground), and also the ruins of Achallader Castle, the ancient stronghold of the Fletchers, once the dominant clan in Glen Orchy. One may derive some idea of what sheep-farming in these wilds entails when one is told that it takes seven or eight shepherds and twice as many sheep-dogs an average of sixteen hours to gather the sheep pastured on no more than *one* hirsel—the feeding-place of one particular flock— among the 33,000 acres comprising merely the sheep-farm of Achallader. And, since there are several hirsels, the ingathering extends over several days. In wet or misty weather it may occupy weeks. The outlying hirsels, where the snows often linger long after lambing-time, demand from shepherds and dogs a degree of physical endurance of which only those born and bred among mountains are capable. Lambing-time at Achallader is always a period of anxiety, especially if snow falls then. Casualties among ewes and lambs may be heavy. The farmhouse now becomes a place of perpetual activity. Breakfasts begin about 1 a.m.; and meals are being served all day long, and well into the night, for conditions may be such as render it impossible for this shepherd or that to say when he may be expected back from the hills. He may have to carry home with him, a distance of several miles, a new-born lamb or two which have lost their mothers. The mothers may have perished in the snows; and their lambs are too delicate to be left outside. They are brought home, and placed in a wooden box by the kitchen fire in the farmhouse. There they are nurtured by feeding-bottles. Strong men have perished among the mountains about Achallader.

41

ROMANTIC LOCH EIL

No LESS alluring than the Road to the Isles—that which runs by Ailort and by Morar to the sea—is the road which, at the head of Loch Eil, branches off in the direction of Ardgour and Sunart, Ardnamurchan and Moidart. Loch Eil, situated partly in Argyll, and partly on the mutual border of that shire and Inverness-shire, is one of the most romantic of the sea-lochs on the Western Highlands. The countryside in which it lies is steeped in clan history and in romance. In olden times it was the patrimony of the royalist Clan Cameron; and to this day it has remained the homeland of many of this time-honoured name. The Camerons' sacrifices for the cause of the Old and the Young Chevalier (so frequently miscalled the Old and the Young Pretender) have won for their patronymic a deep and undying affection among the more discerning readers of the history of the Highlands.

IN NORTHERN ARGYLL

THE road to Moidart leads past the Corran Narrows (*above*), between Ardgour and Lochaber. When the tide in Loch Linnhe is at the turn this is indeed a fascinating spot, especially when the summer sun rides overhead, and one or more vessels are passing through the Narrows on their way to or from Fort William, twelve miles farther up the loch. By the time one has reached the trim village of Ardgour itself, and is approaching the lovely beech avenue beyond it, the call of Ardnamurchan and of Clan Ranald's Moidart becomes irresistible. A sideways glance through the beeches affords some exquisite glimpses of the Appin coast and of the mountains of Glen Coe. On a rocky promontory in Ardnamurchan, overshadowed by Ben Hiant, are the massive ruins of Mingary Castle (*below*), where King James IV of Scotland held court in 1495, and was pleased to accept even the nominal submission of the lawless chiefs of the Western Highlands and Islands. Mingary in ancient days was the stronghold of the MacIans of Ardnamurchan, a branch of the Clan Donald.

BUSY TOWNS OF THE WESTERN HIGHLANDS

WITH the increasing popularity of the Western Highlands, Fort William and Mallaig have become centres of considerable activity, especially during the tourist season. All day long in summer and autumn the pier at the former (*above*) is thronged with passengers arriving or leaving by steamer. Fort William itself had its origin in the fort built by General Monk in Cromwellian times, with a view to quelling the rebellious Highlanders. The fort was reconstructed during the reign of William III, which explains the town's name. In later years the fort was of considerable service to the Hanoverians during the Jacobite Risings. In 1894, when the West Highland Railway was extended to Fort William, it was demolished to make room for engine sheds and a locomotive yard. All that was left standing was the Governor's House, which, until 1935, accommodated some of the railway staff. In 1938 even this old building was taken down—but not before the Governor's Room, panelled in Scots pine, had been removed and re-erected in the West Highland Museum, no distance away. The extension of the railway to Mallaig necessitated the construction there of the piers at which one now embarks for so many of the Inner and Outer Hebrides. These piers in recent years have acquired additional importance through the development of Mallaig as a fishing port. Throughout the fishing season, herring-drifters (*right*) land their catches within a hundred yards of a railhead in direct communication with London.

44

REMINDERS OF THE '45

AT GLENFINNAN, by the head of Loch Shiel, in western Inverness-shire, stands a tall column (*left*) surmounted by a statue of Prince Charlie. It commemorates the unfurling on this spot, on 19 August, 1745, of the Jacobite Standard, at the inauguration of "The Forty-five." This memorial, known popularly as Prince Charlie's Monument, was erected early in the nineteenth century by Alexander MacDonald of Glenaladale, in memory of the inviolable fidelity of his forefathers, and of the rest of those who perished in that arduous and unfortunate enterprise. Just three weeks prior to the raising of the Standard, Prince Charlie, accompanied by a small band of his more intimate associates, landed secretly from France on the shore of *Loch nan Uamh*, Loch of the Caves (*top, right*). The cave by the shore of this loch in which they concealed themselves is still pointed out. It was one of the many in this neighbourhood to which the Prince had to resort after the defeat of his army at Culloden, the following April. Among the remotest is that (*bottom, right*) situated high upon the hillside above Loch Beoraid. So concealed is its entrance by birch and mountain ash that it is often difficult to locate. It was among these wilds that the Prince, a hunted fugitive, wandered for months. But one day news reached him that a French frigate had arrived for him. So he returned to Clan Ranald's house at Borrodale (*centre, right*), there to await an opportunity for escape. That frigate bore him away from Scotland for ever. Preserved in one of the rooms at Borrodale House is a fragment of wallpaper no larger than a man's hand. It is all that remains of the paper covering the wall of this apartment when it was occupied by the hapless Prince.

LOCH EARN, PERTHSHIRE

AMONG the largest lochs in Perthshire is Loch Earn. Hollowed out of the solid rock by glaciation, it is a true rock basin, six miles in length, with an average width of three-quarters of a mile and a maximum depth of 287 feet. During the period of greatest glaciation the ice-sheet crossed this region in an east-south-easterly direction, exerting its greatest pressure on the south side of the valley, which it scooped out.

The Central Highlands

THE Central Highlands comprise an astonishing variety of general characteristics and natural conditions. For our immediate purpose they include those parts of Dunbartonshire and of Stirlingshire bordering Loch Lomond, the very beautiful county of Perth, and the comparatively infertile county of Inverness, excluding from the last mentioned, of course, those western regions already dealt with in the previous section. The area now under review embraces a considerable portion of the Grampians, together with other mountain groups, such as the Arrochar Hills, the Sidlaws, most of the Ochils, the Monadhliath and the more westerly of the Cairngorms. It also includes that splendid assortment of east-flowing rivers. The Tay, Scotland's longest river, flows through it. So, also, does the Forth; while in the central fastnesses of Inverness-shire, and at a little loch of the same name, the incontinent Spey has its birth.

More than half of Scotland's—nay, of Britain's—best known lochs likewise occur in this region: Loch Lomond and Loch Katrine, Loch Arklet, Loch Ard, Loch Achray and Loch Vennachar, Loch Earn and Loch Tay, Loch Tummel and Loch Rannoch, Loch Ericht and Loch Laggan, and, of course, Loch Ness, whose monster is still being seen.

Perthshire lies in the middle of Scotland. But for the Carse of Gowrie (that fertile stretch of alluvial flat between the Sidlaws and the North Sea) it is entirely an inland county. Its western reaches are almost as sterile as its central and eastern are fertile. How varied a region it is cannot be demonstrated in words more apt than those Sir Walter Scott employs in *The Fair Maid of Perth*. "Amid all the provinces of Scotland," he writes, "if an intelligent stranger were asked to describe the most varied and the most beautiful, it is probable he would name the county of Perth. A native also of any other district of Caledonia, though his partialities might lead him to prefer his native county in the first instance, would certainly class that of Perth in the second, and thus give its inhabitants a fair right to plead that—prejudice apart—Perthshire forms the fairest portion of the northern kingdom."

The Lowland parts of the county, particularly the valley of Strathmore and the Carse, are noted for their fertility. Yet it must be mentioned that only a fifth of its area is under cultivation, and that it is very doubtful how much of the remainder is capable of producing a grain or a green crop of any kind, except at an expenditure of money and labour out of all proportion to the value of what might be raised on it. If this be true of Perthshire, it is even more so of Inverness-shire, most of which consists of mountain and moorland.

Perthshire's position at the very heart of Scotland has made it the scene of many of that country's most stirring events. It would be no exaggeration to say that every town, village, and hamlet, every loch and river, has its historical associations. One has but to scan the place-names occurring in Professor Hume Brown's *History of Scotland* to realize how large a proportion of them belongs to a county which, in the less orderly centuries, was something of a cockpit. How many battles between Highlanders and Lowlanders were fought within its confines!

No county in Britain affords scenery grander and more romantic than Perthshire's. Its lofty mountains, its numerous rivers with their falls, its woodlands, its farm-lands and its croft-lands, all combine to produce a landscape which the world has revered ever since the Wizard of the North laid it out so perfectly on the printed page. Who has not heard of the Trossachs, and of the rest of the MacGregor Country impinging upon it? Who has not read of Rob Roy's exploits among the fastnesses of Loch Lomond, or in ambush among the quieter lanes about Aberfoyle? It is, indeed, remarkable that one so rebellious should have died peaceably in his own bed, and been buried in orthodox fashion.

If the memory of Rob lingers in Perthshire, that of Bonnie Prince Charlie does so in Inverness-shire, for this was the county with which his enterprises were most closely identified. He landed from France on its wild, west coast, hopeful and ardent. He left for ever from the same loch-side as had first felt his princely feet when he came to redeem what his autocratic ancestors had forfeited. Gay and hopeful at Glenfinnan among such of the clans as had answered his rallying-call, a few months later he was to lose all at Drummossie Muir—at Culloden—on the other side of this vast county. Its cavernous mountains and shores were afterwards to shelter him as a fugitive. One scents a whiff of "The Forty-five" as distinctly about the town of Inverness and its environs as one does in those western seaboard retreats.

The extent to which the wilds of the Central Highlands harboured those in rebellion for the Old Chevalier and, later, for his son, the Young Chevalier, was shown by the Hanoverians' determination to bring them under central control. This, they realized, could only be done by making them accessible to marching regiments. And so General Wade pursued in these regions his vast road-making enterprises, carrying the war well into the rebels' fastnesses.

It may not be inappropriate to say, in conclusion, that, whatever may have been the virtues or the shortcomings of the Stewarts, there was absolutely no *pretence* about their claim to the throne. The terms, Old Pretender and Young Pretender, are therefore quite misleading. There was nothing of Lambert Simnel about Old James, nothing of Perkin Warbeck about Young Charles.

SUMMER MORNING ON LOCH LOMOND

THE view from Inversnaid across Loch Lomond, toward Ardlui and the Arrochar Hills, on a calm, summery morning, suggests something temporarily wrested from Faerie, so remarkably lovely is it. By the shore there, and reached by a road falling very steeply from Glen Arklet, stands the hostelry at which many a famous traveller has sojourned. Nearby the Snaid Burn tumbles to the loch in the waterfall of which the poets have sung.

RELICS OF A LESS PEACEFUL AGE

IN GLEN ARKLET, not far from the point where the Arklet Water leaves the loch of the same name to topple into Loch Lomond at Inversnaid, stood the fort known as the Inversnaid Garrison, built about the time of the Rebellion of 1715. Nearby is the burying-ground of the soldiers who died there during the years that the Garrison was occupied. The Hanoverians at this time were concerned not only with keeping an eye on the disaffected clans in the neighbourhood, but also with curbing the arbitrary activities of Rob Roy MacGregor and his wild Highlandmen. Rob once owned property at Inversnaid. His differences with the Duke of Montrose led to the confiscation of this property, to the burning of his home, and largely to the building and garrisoning of the fort at Inversnaid, in the hope that it might place some check upon his lawless enterprises. The ruins of the Garrison are now incorporated in the steading and other outbuildings at the Garrison Farm, seen in the middle distance, to the right of the picture. Indeed, most of them are now used as sheep-pens. Only the tops of the stones marking the graves of those who died at the Garrison are visible today, above the grass and moss. In this old burial-place is a large memorial stone erected by Montrose to those soldiers who died at Inversnaid. Local tradition declares that among the first to be placed in command of the Garrison was Captain Wolfe, who afterwards conquered Quebec. When Sir Walter Scott passed this way toward the close of the eighteenth century he was struck by the change that fifty years had wrought. The garrison had diminished to a single veteran. This old man was busy on his croft when Scott arrived, and told him that the key of the fort might be found under the door.

LOCH LOMONDSIDE

ONE questions whether there exists anywhere a freshwater lake, the shores of which are as rich in historic, romantic, and literary associations as are the shores of Loch Lomond. From the River Leven, its outlet, where so many houseboats (*below*) are moored, to its farthest reach, where the Falloch enters at the foot of the glen of the same name, its shores ring with the romances and the tragedies of Buchanans, Campbells, Colquhouns, Grahams, MacFarlanes, MacGregors, and Murrays. In olden times the lands of many of these warlike clans impinged upon the Bonnie, Bonnie Banks. Not far from the head of the loch is the Pulpit Rock (*right*), so called because of the cavity cut out of it, from which a minister used to preach to his congregation seated in front.

THE PASS OF LENY AND LOCH KATRINE

Two and a half miles west of the Perthshire village of Callander is the famous Pass of Leny, through which flows the River Leny (*left*) from Loch Lubnaig, on its way to join the Teith. Scott describes the Pass in *The Legend of Montrose*. It is flanked by wooded precipices, and is overhung on its west side by the stern acclivities of Ben Ledi (2,875 feet). In ancient days the Pass was one of the principal gateways to the Highlands. So easily was it defended that a handful of resolute clansmen could have held up an army attempting to enter by it. Of all the lochs of Perthshire none exceeds in loveliness and romantic association Loch Katrine, at the east end of which lie the Trossachs, and at its narrow, western extremity Glen Gyle, birthplace of the author's ancestor, Rob Roy MacGregor. One of the best known of Loch Katrine's many famed prospects is that from the Lady's Rock (*above*). Though readers of *The Lady of the Lake* now look in vain for the Silver Strand, they will experience little difficulty in locating in this colourful countryside most of the other scenes and settings of which the Wizard wrote so intimately. Ellen's Isle is still there. So, too, are the Pass of the Cattle, known to the caterans of old, and the lofty peaks of Ben Venue and Ben A'n, between which the Trossachs actually lie. Scott was the first to bring to public notice the beauty and historical romance of Loch Katrine and the Trossachs.

WINTER IN GLEN GYLE

AT THE head of Loch Katrine lies the sweet, secluded valley known as Glen Gyle (pictured here in early winter), once part of the vast patrimony of the Clan Gregor. There, in the old house of Glen Gyle, in 1671, was born Rob Roy, one of the most notable of the MacGregors. The house was burnt down at least twice—once in 1716, when three separate parties, organized in Stirling, Perth, and Glasgow respectively, set out "toward the house and haunts of the notorious robber and rebel, Robert Roy MacGregor." Among the trees sheltering the present Glen Gyle House is the ivied burying-ground of the author's ancestors, the MacGregors of Glen Gyle. Successive raisings of the level of Loch Katrine, in order to amplify Glasgow's water supply, have inundated most of Glen Gyle's pastures.

HIGHLAND ANTIQUITIES

ON EACH side of the entrance to the roofless Auld Kirk at Aberfoyle, in Perthshire, lies an iron mort-safe (*above, left*), reminiscent of "resurrectionist" days in Scotland, when surgeons, for dissecting purposes, paid good prices for good corpses! In the old kirkyard at Rothiemurchus, in Inverness-shire, is the recumbent slab marking the grave of Farquhar Shaw, who died in 1405. On the slab are five queer stones (*above, right*) which, according to tradition, appear and disappear with the flow and ebb of the fortunes of Rothiemurchus's lairds. On Inch Gailleach, an island in Loch Lomond, is an ancient MacGregor burying-place containing a large tombstone (*below, left*) known as the Grey Stane of Inch Gailleach, upon which, in olden times, were taken the most sacred and binding of oaths. In the old kirkyard at Balquhidder (*below, right*), in the heart of the MacGregor Country, Rob Roy MacGregor and his kindred lie peacefully buried.

MOUNTAIN AND RIVER IN ABERFOYLE

BEN VENUE, seen from Achray in time of snow and ice (*right*), enjoys a splendour truly Alpine. This peak, situated in the Aberfoyle parish of Perthshire, rises from the margin of Loch Katrine. The vast expanse of mountainous, as well as of silvan, territory visible from its summit includes almost the whole of that romantic country covered by *The Lady of the Lake*, wherein Scott has nobly enshrined Ben Venue's rugged and primeval grandeur. In olden times all traffic from the south approached Aberfoyle by the Stockie Muir road, passing through Drymen and Dalmary and Gartmore. It forded the Black Pow, and soon thereafter came under the shadow—and, indeed, the influence—of the Faery Hillock, skirting the knoll on which stands the manse of Aberfoyle. A few hundred yards farther on it crossed the Avon Dubh (the old name of the River Forth) by the old bridge (*below*), now seldom used except by local traffic consisting of farm carts, shepherds with their flocks, and silvicultural workers, afoot, or in vehicles belonging to the Forestry Commission, which for some years now has been occupied with afforestation in this locality. Quite near the bridge is the Auld Kirk of Aberfoyle, where the Rev. Robert Kirk was once minister. It was he who, about the year 1691, wrote *The Secret Commonwealth of Elves, Faunes, and Faeries*. In 1692 he disappeared mysteriously from Aberfoyle, and was believed to have been spirited away to Faerieland, whence, as yet, he has not returned.

BLAIR CASTLE

WITHIN a mile of the Perthshire village of Blair-Atholl stands Blair Castle, seat of the Duke of Atholl. This sturdy, four-storeyed mansion, battlemented and turreted in the Scots Baronial fashion, was restored in 1872. Comyn's Tower, its oldest part, is said to have been built in 1269. The Castle is rich in historic associations. Both James V and his unfortunate daughter, Mary of Scotland, knew it when they went a-hunting in Glen Tilt. Here, in 1644, Montrose mustered his three thousand Atholl Highlanders, whom he marched to victory at Tippermuir. Nine years later the Cromwellian officer, Colonel Daniel, "destroyed by powder" the old keep. In 1689 it was garrisoned by Claverhouse— by Bonnie Dundee—whose body was brought back to it after his success at Killiecrankie, to be buried in the old church cf Blair. In the autumn of 1745 the Young Chevalier spent three nights at Blair Castle. The following spring it was besieged by Jacobite forces commanded by the redoubtable Lord George Murray, brother of the Duke of Atholl.

COMRIE VILLAGE

ON THE left bank of the River Earn, in the heart of that part of Perthshire known as Strathearn, lies the little town of Comrie. Though well known as a summer resort, it is much better known as a place where earthquakes occur more frequently than anywhere else in Britain. Scotland consists of three main regions—the Highlands, the Southern Uplands, and, between these, the Central Valley or Lowlands. Each of these has its own geological characteristics. The boundary line between the Highlands and the Lowlands is a great geological fault. This fault crosses Scotland diagonally, from coast to coast, in a south-westerly–north-easterly direction. Along this line of fault seismological disturbance is quite common, particularly at Comrie, which actually lies on it. There, in 1875, one of the earliest of reliable seismographs was established. It recorded faithfully the several shocks which the village experienced the next year. Comrie is the focus, as it were, of all earth movements in this region. An earth tremor here is always a matter of public interest.

CONTRASTS IN RIVERS

THROUGH Perthshire, in an easterly direction, flow several famous rivers, among them the Tay, Scotland's longest river. It rises in a corrie near the county's confines with Argyll, at an altitude of nearly three thousand feet above sea-level, falling five hundred feet as the Fillan Water in its first eleven miles to Loch Dochart, through which it passes on to Loch Iubhair. For the next fifteen miles or so, and until it enters Loch Tay at Killin, it is known as the Dochart. Just above Killin village are the Falls of Dochart (*left*), where it roars its course over rocks and boulders, diverted this way and that by tree-clad islets lying in mid-stream. The Tay's length from source to mouth is about a hundred and seventeen miles. The River Garry, issuing from the loch of the same name, runs twenty-two miles in an east-south-easterly direction. Below the celebrated Pass of Killiecrankie it falls into the Tummel. In its upper reaches it is one of the most impetuous of British rivers. Just before it arrives at the village of Blair-Atholl (*below*) it slows down, flowing so quietly thereafter, through pastures and woodlands, in its old age.

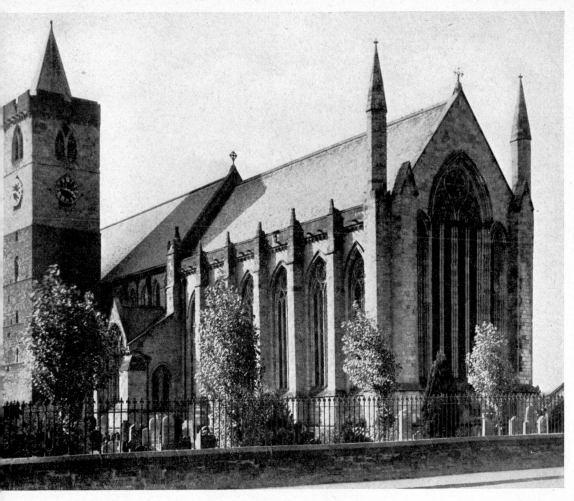

DUNBLANE CATHEDRAL

ON THE left bank of the Allan Water, five miles north of Stirling, stands the ancient city of Dunblane—a city only in name, for it is but a little, Highland town, the main street of which, composed mostly of old houses, is both narrow and crooked. Of its antiquity, however, there is no doubt. Invaders from Strathclyde burned it about the middle of the ninth century. Early in the tenth the Danes ravaged it. Its church, founded by St. Blane, pre-dates these calamities. It belongs to the seventh century. The bishopric of Dunblane dates from about the middle of the twelfth century, being one of the later bishoprics established by the "Sair Sanct for the Croun"—David I. One of its earliest bishops was Maurice—he who, as chaplain to Robert the Bruce, blessed the Scottish Army at Bannockburn. In post-Reformation times the saintly Bishop Leighton selected Dunblane as the smallest and most impoverished see in Scotland. There he ministered for nine years, until his translation, in 1670, to the Archbishopric of Glasgow. His fervent association with Dunblane is perpetuated in the Bishop's Well, in the Bishop's Walk by the romantic Allan Water, and in the Leightonian Library. Dunblane's fame resides largely in its Cathedral, the choir of which, since the Reformation, has served as the parish church (*above*). It was of Dunblane Cathedral that Archbishop Laud remarked in 1633 that "this was a goodly church before the *De*formation." Its glory was—and, indeed, still is—its west front. "Do you recollect the West Window of your own Dunblane Cathedral?" Ruskin asked an Edinburgh audience. "It is acknowledged to be beautiful by the most careless observer."

THE CHANGING HIGHLANDS: DAM AND CAB

DEEP set among the mountains in the Arrochar parish of Dunbartonshire is Loch Sloy. Here, in recent years, the merest strip of tarn, shut in between Ben Vorlich and Ben Vane, has been dammed to form one of the largest hydro-electric reservoirs in the country. The loch's overflow was the Inveruglas Water, bickering down Glen Sloy to join the upper waters of Loch Lomond. Today the Inveruglas Water has to be content with what is known as compensation water. Today, moreover, the dams, pylons and cables, tunnels and turbines of the great Loch Sloy hydro-electric scheme characterize a region once so remote and picturesque. From the thirteenth century until the eighteenth all this watershed, and much territory on every side of it, belonged to the Clan MacFarlane. Loch Sloy was its gathering-place. From it the clan took its *sluagh-ghairm*, its war-cry or slogan —*Loch Sluagh*—Loch Sloy—Loch of the Hosts. What may have happened to the Faerie

A GREAT HYDRO-ELECTRIC SCHEME

Dyers of Inveruglas since the electricians invaded their province so purposefully, no one can tell. But the water of the little loch in the *Lag Uaine*, the Green Hollow, they say, still retains the wonderful green colour said to have been imparted to it when the Little Folk of the Lennox had their dyeing works away up there, and the Clan MacFarlane's midnight raids on the territories of neighbouring clans gave to the moon the title of "MacFarlane's Lantern." In May, 1948, at the age of ninety-six, the late Miss Mary MacFarlane, grandniece of the Highland Girl at Inversnaid, whom Wordsworth immortalized, switched on, from her bath-chair, the electric power derived from Loch Sloy for the village of Arrochar, after a ceremony held at "Bellevue," her cottage there. It was indeed appropriate that, under her aged hand, "MacFarlane's Lantern," so long the terror of this countryside, should have acquired a significance so orderly and so peaceful.

LOCH FASKALLY

THIS quiet corner of Faskally, in Perthshire, shows the care taken by the builders of the hydro-electric installations to preserve the amenities of the countryside. Loch Faskally is an artificial lake formed by the flooding of a stretch of the River Tummel in connection with the Tummel-Garry scheme. In this scene of placid beauty the authorities have made available facilities for boating, and for trout and salmon fishing, organized by a committee of local people. As far as possible, all the buildings and embankments of the hydro-electric schemes, as also the houses of resident staff, are built of local stone. Soil is laid and grass sown on the spoil tips and building sites, to cover the scars caused during construction.

FISH PASS AT PITLOCHRY

WHERE salmon rivers have had to be dammed for hydro-electric purposes, fish passes have had to be built to allow the fish to travel upstream to spawn. In order to ensure that such rivers continue to flow, compensation water is provided. This means that water flows continuously through the fish passes, thus attracting the fish to their spawning beds. Such a pass is to be seen at Pitlochry, as part of the Tummel-Garry scheme. The installations there were visited during 1951 by more than ten thousand people. The Pitlochry dam is fifty feet high; and the fish pass rises in steps of eighteen inches. From an observation chamber, in 1951, five thousand six hundred salmon were seen running upstream to spawn.

CASTLES OF THE CENTRAL HIGHLANDS

ON AN islet in Loch an Eilein, in the Rothiemurchus district of Inverness-shire, stand the ruins of an old keep (*top, left*) said to have been the retreat of Alexander Stewart, Earl of Buchan, the lawless brother of King Robert, and better known to history as the Wolf of Badenoch—the villain who set fire to Elgin Cathedral. The story of his association with this keep seems to have been invented, either by Sir Walter Scott or by Sir Thomas Dick Lauder. Its ruins are said to have been the last nesting-place in Scotland of the osprey. One of the most interesting edifices in Nairnshire is Cawdor Castle (*centre, left*), perched on the rocky brow of the Cawdor Burn, in the midst of venerable trees. The nucleus of the present castle was built about the middle of the fifteenth century. The Calders of Calder were said to be descended from a brother of Macbeth, to whom, on his assumption of the crown, he resigned the thanedom of Cawdor. In ancient days the castle was a place of vast strength. Tradition tells of its having been the hiding-place, after Culloden, of Lord Lovat. On an eminence about the centre of the Highland town of Inverness, with the River Ness flowing broadly below its western side (*bottom, left*), is Inverness Castle, built in the Tudor castellated style, a structure of red sandstone dating from 1834. It houses the principal county offices. Whether the castle actually stands upon the site of that occupied by Macbeth, the Mormaer of Moray, is a moot point. On the esplanade of the present castle is an imposing memorial to Flora Mac-Donald (the work of Andrew David-son, an Inverness sculptor). One of the principal objects of antiquarian interest in the Loch Ness region of

68

Inverness-shire is Castle Urquhart (*above*), the ruins of which stand prominently on a point jutting out into Loch Ness. The original castle on this site was built in the twelfth century. This Edward I, the veritable Hammer of the Scots, besieged and took, ultimately replacing it by a fortress, the crumbling ruins of which we now see by the shores of Loch Ness. In the Killin parish of Perthshire, at the head of Loch Tay, are the ruins of Finlarig Castle (*right*), an ancient seat of the Campbells of Breadalbain. Here, in this narrow, three-storeyed, ivied place of strength, with its square tower at one corner, according to Sir Walter Scott's *The Fair Maid of Perth*, died the chief of the Clan Quhele. Near at hand is a family vault of the Breadalbains. Finlarig lies in the heart of territory that knew much turbulence in the long-forgotten days of clan warfare.

69

THE PASS OF KILLIECRANKIE

THE Pass of Killiecrankie, in Perthshire, is one of the sublimest of the many defiles that in olden times provided the Highlanders with strategic points at which they could resist, with comparative ease, the invasion of their territory, either by the Lowland Scots or by the English. Today the Pass is traversed not only by the River Garry, which formed it, but also by the main road and the main railway reaching far into northern Scotland. In the days of William III it was deemed the most perilous of all the treacherous ravines from which the Highland marauders were wont to sally forth upon the fertile farm-lands of the Lowlands. On a small plain at the head of the Pass, near Killiecrankie railway station, was fought, on 27 July, 1689, the celebrated conflict in which Graham of Claverhouse—"Bonnie Dundee" —defeated King William's troops under General MacKay, though Claverhouse lost his life.

GATHERING OF A HIGHLAND CLAN

BADENOCH is the name given to the south-eastern district of Inverness-shire, through which runs a considerable stretch of the impetuous Spey. Most of it, in olden days, was owned by the Earls of Huntly and their successors, the Dukes of Gordon. The upper part, however, has long been the patrimony of the Clan MacPherson. One recalls in this connection the exploits of Cluny MacPherson, Chief of the Clan—better known perhaps as "Cluny of The Forty-Five"—on behalf of Prince Charlie. The Prince, during his fugitive wanderings, spent an uncomfortable night or two at "a very romantic and comical habitation made by Cluny," at a high and wellnigh inaccessible spot on Ben Alder known as Cluny's Cage. This picture shows members of the MacPherson Clan marching behind their pipe band at their first annual rally, at Newtonmore, in the heart of the Clan country, in 1947.

CLUNY MacPherson frequented many a place of refuge in the Highland hills besides his Cage; and among the safest was that near Dalchully, not far from the upper reaches of the Spey (*above*), and at no great distance from the military road General Wade and his Hanoverian soldiery built between Dalwhinnie and Fort Augustus, traversing in its loftiest altitudes the famous Pass of Corrieyarrick. Throughout this countryside, even at the present day, considerable stretches of Wade's roads, where they have not been absorbed in the highways of later years, are easily traced. Moreover, many of the bridges he built to carry these roads across the Highland rivers and burns still exist. A splendid example may be seen crossing the Dulnain, a tributary of the Spey, at Sluggan (*left*), in the heart of Inverness-shire. Just before the Second World War the author happened to be approaching this bridge, now used but seldom, when he noticed, ahead of him, a number of cavalrymen on grey steeds. They were a contingent of the

72

HLAND ROADS

Scots Greys, riding picturesquely through this countryside on a recruiting campaign. Appropriately enough, they crossed the Dulnain at Sluggan, by Wade's old bridge. At Garva, in 1732, Wade carried his Corrieyarrick road across the Spey by the double-arched bridge known as St. George's Bridge (*above*), a structure a hundred and fifty feet in length, each of its arches spanning forty feet to the centre pier erected on a rock in the middle of the river. Small by comparison is the bridge (*right*) bearing this same road over the mountain stream called the Yarrick, high up in the Pass. Wade's Corrieyarrick road fell into desuetude toward the close of the nineteenth century. The year 1890 was the last in which horses were brought over this famous Pass to the Falkirk Trysts. The last cattle were driven along this road in 1896, and the last sheep in 1899. Little did its promoters and builders imagine that it was ever likely to be of service to the Jacobites in the moving of *their* troops, or in providing secure entrenchments along its sides.

73

THE PINE-WOODS OF ROTHIEMURCHUS

THREE-FOURTHS of the shores of Loch an Eilein, in Rothiemurchus, are fringed with pine-trees, right down to the water's edge. For anyone unaccustomed to scenes of this kind, the extent and density of these pines, comprising the Forest of Rothiemurchus, would be difficult to comprehend. They sweep away and away beyond Loch an Eilein to an altitude on the northern flanks of the Cairngorms, above which they find it hard to survive in any numbers. It is doubtful whether there exists anywhere else in Britain so extensive an area covered with pines sown by nature; and there are few scenes more inspiring than that from the birch-clad crags of the Ord Ban, depicted above. In the foreground is Loch an Eilein, with its islet and ruined keep. Beyond stretch the vast and dark forests, backed by the Cairngorms. The highest point in the picture is the summit of Cairngorm itself (4,084 feet).

IN WILD GLEN TRUIM

No LESS arduous an undertaking than Wade's road over the Corrieyarrick was the road he constructed between Dunkeld and Inverness, threading its way past Pitlochry and Blair Atholl, thence through Glen Garry and the Pass of Drumuachdar, following closely thereafter the course of the Truim (*below*) to Invernahavon, where that river joins the Spey, six miles south-west of Kingussie, and where, in 1370, was fought that sanguinary battle between the MacPhersons and the Camerons. Glen Truim, where today road, rail, and river travel close to one another, is wild and mountainous, and much exposed in time of snow. Here and there, on both sides of the railway line, may be seen rows of sleepers set up on end to prevent what is by no means an unusual occurrence in this region, namely, the interruption of rail communication between Perth and Inverness by snowdrifts across the track.

INVERNESS, situated on the east and the west banks of the River Ness, not far from where that short and broad river enters the Beauly Firth, an arm of the extensive Moray Firth, is surely one of the most beautifully placed towns in Britain. It lies at the north-eastern extremity of the Great Glen of Scotland, which, after leaving that part of it in which is situated Loch Ness, begins to widen out into a fertile plain as it approaches the eastern seaboard. The town's environs are particularly lovely; and of the scenery beyond, innumerable travellers have written with enthusiasm. One recalls, in this context, that memorable passage from Dr. MacCulloch's *Letters on the Highlands*: "When I have stood in Queen Street of Edinburgh and looked towards Fife, I have sometimes wondered whether Scotland contained a finer view of its class. But I have forgotten this on my arrival at Inverness. Surely,

THE HIGHLANDS

if a comparison is to be made with Edinburgh, always excepting its own romantic disposition, the Firth of Forth must yield the palm to the Moray Firth, the surrounding country must yield altogether, and Inverness must take the highest rank. Everything is done, too, for Inverness that can be effected by wood and cultivation; the characters of which, here, have altogether a richness, a variety, and a freedom which we miss round Edinburgh. The mountain screens are finer, more varied, and more near. Each outlet is different from the other; and each is beautiful." The High Street of Inverness (*left*), indeed a busy thoroughfare on a market day, is dominated by the tall steeple with its bells, and the Town Clock. The river is a never-ending joy, lending to the town a unique loveliness, whether in time of flood or of drought. In summer children can often wade across it with ease and in safety.

77

BUT six miles from Inverness lies Culloden Moor, anciently known as Drummossie. Here, on 16 April, 1746, was fought the Battle of Culloden, the last warring contest on British soil. The defeat of Prince Charles Edward and his forces by the Hanoverians, under command of the Duke of Cumberland, sealed the fate of the fateful Stuarts. Culloden was the culmination of the Jacobites' final attempt to regain a throne which they might well have retained had they been less obstinate. The area of the battlefield was acquired by the National Trust for Scotland in various small parcels in 1937 and 1944. It includes the Graves of the Clans, the Graves of the English, the Memorial Cairn (*top, right*), the Well of the Dead, the old King's Stables, the Cumberland Stone (*bottom, right*), and Leanach Farmhouse (*bottom, left*). The last-mentioned, sometimes referred to as Culloden Cottage, is said to have been used by Prince Charlie as his army headquarters. The inscription on the Memorial Cairn bears a wistful poignancy, for, whereas most Scots are Hanoverian at head, they remain Jacobite at heart: "The Battle of Culloden was fought on

this moor 16 April, 1746. The Graves of the Gallant Highlanders who fought for Scotland and Prince Charlie are marked by the names of their Clans." This cairn epitomizes the end of an old order of things, and the death of chivalry as Scotland had known it. With the details of the battle one need not be detained here. Suffice it to remark that on this very moor was enacted a scene that, had fortune favoured otherwise, would undoubtedly have altered the entire trend of British history, and perhaps also of the history of the world. In less than an hour the Jacobites were routed by Hanoverians whose casualties were negligible. Those of the latter who lost their lives were buried near at hand, in that patch of arable ground known ever since as the Field of the English. The vanquished clansmen were buried according to their respective clans, just where they fell. By the Well of the Dead stands a solitary stone marking the spot where the Chief of the Mac-Gillivrays fell. Nearby is the stone (*top, left*) commemorating fallen MacGillivrays, Mac-Leans, MacLachlans, and Atholl Highlanders. Other clans have headstones of their own.

IN THE last eighty years the population of the Highlands has fallen by seventy-five thousand. In their attempts to arrest this decline successive governments in recent years have concerned themselves with the development of the resources of the Highlands, anxious that its inhabitants might attain to a standard of living not inferior to that enjoyed in other parts of the country, and therefore be less inclined to migrate southwards. The utilization of water-power in the generating of electricity, alluded to earlier, will, it is hoped, do something to improve economic standards prevailing hitherto. Plans for preventing a further decline in Highland population also embrace an expansion of the activities of the Forestry Commission, which proposed in 1950 to plant, within the next few years, a further sixty thousand acres in the Highlands alone, permanently employing as many as seven thousand men. During

the first three years of their schemes for expansion the Commission proposed spending on the Highlands a sum exceeding £5,000,000. At the same time it will continue with its policy of assisting private owners to extend their forests. The pictures on these two pages show the Commission's undertaking at Strathyre, Perthshire. Situated close to the railway between Stirling and Oban, as well as to the highroad from Stirling to Lochearnhead, it is seen by many thousands of travellers in the course of a year. The young trees are first raised in the forest nursery (*left*), where larches are in course of being transplanted. More mature plantations of larch and of spruce may be seen on the steep hillside beyond. When the trees are fifteen years old, they are thinned out (*right*). Those to be removed are marked with a notch made in the trunk. The felled trees are made into fencing-posts or into pit-props.

CULLODEN WISHING WELL

To THE Memorial Cairn at Culloden, to the Graves of the vanquished Clans, to the Well of the Dead, and also to the famous Wishing Well (*above*), many thousands of visitors find their way each year. As recently as the first Sunday of May, 1939, a great concourse of people from all over the north of Scotland assembled at the Wishing Well, despite an appeal by the Sabbath Observance Association. On arrival there, many of them carried out the old practice of drinking the water, expressing a wish and dropping a coin into the well. Thereafter the well-wishers tied pieces of cloth to the trees near at hand (*left*), hoping thus to ensure the fulfilment of their wish. When this well was cleaned out a few years ago it yielded coins to the value of nearly thirty pounds sterling.

THE DOUNE OF ROTHIEMURCHUS

IN THE heart of Inverness-shire is the Doune of Rothiemurchus, until a few years ago the home of the Grants of Rothiemurchus. It is situated on level ground amid peaceful surroundings, with a broad prospect of greenery retreating away from its southern windows, sprinkled with fine trees, some of them pine, some of them deciduous. Close at hand the Spey runs through long, dark pools toward Aviemore. The oldest part of the Doune, much of the exterior wall of which is still visible, is indeed interesting. Over the lintel of the doorway, in that part of it built about 1700, is a stone beautifully carved with the motto: "In God is al my Trest," together with various emblems and armorial bearings, and the date 1597. The old house is not without its ghost and its brownie. Long after the inmates were abed, the latter could be heard in the kitchen, washing up the dishes and tinkering the pots and pans.

LOCH STACK

IF ONE follow to the western seaboard the road traversing wild Sutherland past Lochs Shin, Merkland, and More, one comes at length to Loch Stack, a smaller loch than any of these. It is overshadowed by two peaks—Arcuil (or Arkle) to the north, Ben Stack to the south-west. Out of this loch flows the Laxford, famous for its salmon and trout fishing, a distance of nearly six miles to the head of the sea-loch of the same name, among the wildest scenery.

The North-western
Highlands

FOR our present purpose this section comprises that part of the Scottish Highlands included in Wester Ross and western and north-western Sutherland. Although those districts of the former situated south of Kyle of Lochalsh are now comparatively easy of access by road, the greater part of the latter remains inaccessible, especially in winter-time, when for weeks on end it may be completely cut off, except perhaps to the hardiest and most adventurous of travellers, either afoot or awheel. In time of heavy and persistent snow, few attempt to reach it or to quit it.

The entire region is extremely mountainous—so much so that, when viewed in panorama from one of its innumerable summits, it would appear to consist of wild, chaotic mountains, steep valleys, and deep, sinister lochs, to the exclusion of territory upon which ordinary mortals could live and move and have their being.

The distances are great. Many of them cannot be travelled except on foot. Accommodation is found only with difficulty, as might well be expected in a region which, in relation to area, is by far the most sparsely populated in Britain. Yet these wilds are imbued with something. They have their own allure, particularly for him who would venture forth in country untamed and largely undiscovered. The man of solitary disposition will welcome what the more social will deplore— the lack of roads, along which he may motor at any rate to within a mile or two of his objective. Here the true mountaineer or the sturdy walker on broken ground is provided with all the tests he requires. Those isolated peaks of Ross and of Sutherland—the Coigach group, for instance, or perhaps Suilven—have no easy approach. They are trackless except where the timid deer have worn a thread upon the moorlands and the hillsides and the sliding screes. Patient and laborious footslogging over miles of country indescribably lonely and remote is the only thing which will bring one to one's destination hereabouts. The mountaineer, making his assault on our north-western peaks as weather conditions will allow, does so in the knowledge that his attaining his objective is truly something in the nature of adventure. He is indeed on a first-class expedition.

The very remoteness of this region delayed long any accurate and comprehensive data on its topography and geology. The former is intricate, though perhaps

85

not so much so as the latter. Geologists, attracted by mountain formations as unique in shape as they are in composition, have now reduced this complex area, after much commendable application and physical hardship. The mountains of Torridonian sandstone, capped by Cambrian quartzite, such as is to be found in the Loch Maree neighbourhood, in Assynt, and, of course, in Torridon itself, presented problems hitherto unknown to the field geologist.

It might be said, moreover, that here the hill-climber finds something entirely different from what he has been accustomed to. Where, in Britain, is there a mountain more remarkable, more fantastic, than Stack Polly, or Suilven, the Grey Castle? Where are there corries finer than those of Beinn Eighe, or of An Teallach? The coastline, entered by several sea-lochs primeval in their splendour and aloofness, is barren and rugged. The Norwegian fiords afford scenery no grander. As the hinterland is composed almost entirely of mountain and loch, moorland and bog, slithering screes and precipitous streams, it is uninhabitable except for the few gamekeepers and foresters dwelling remotely at such places as Aultnacealgach, the tiny hamlet by the lone road to Lochinver, in the heart of the Sutherland wastes. Here, in the sense in which Edward FitzGerald meant it, a few meagre strips of herbage grown divide the desert from the sown.

At various points along the coast, and often at the head of the sea-lochs, are the little crofts of those who inhabit this inhospitable land. The stranger, discovering them for the first time, is amazed. Unaware of the spell that binds the northern Celt to his meagre tenure, he wonders why anyone rational should want to live so remotely, so precariously, so penuriously. Most of us have asked ourselves this question after seeing such scenes in the summer or autumn months, when they are at their brightest and best. Imagine them in the dead of winter, frequently cut off for several consecutive weeks by sea as well as by land! Take, for example, the country about Applecross, which is one of the wildest, though the name certainly suggests something of sunshine and orchard. Thomas Pennant described it aptly as "most uncommonly mountainous." The railway approaches no nearer than Kyle of Lochalsh. Six days a week the mail-steamer sailing from that rail-head to Stornoway, in the Outer Hebrides, is due to call on her outward voyage each afternoon, and again on her inward voyage the following morning. Though Applecross Bay is sheltered by comparison with the waters she traverses beyond Skye, it may be too stormy for the Applecross ferryboat to make contact with her. The alternative overland communication is by way of the celebrated Pass of the Cattle, one of the highest and most formidable mountain-roads in Britain.

The peculiar remoteness of many of the districts covered by this section is shown by the fact that even today the inhabitants are variously nicknamed. Those of Lochcarron, for instance, are called, in Gaelic, the Black Ravens. Those of Loch Broom are known as the Buzzards: those of Gairloch as the Cods.

WEAVING TWEED NEAR LOCH CARRON

THE considerable success in recent years of the Harris tweed industry in the Highlands and Islands of Scotland, where hand-loom weaving has been increasing in answer to a rising demand for its product, has done much to alleviate economic conditions which may well return if the wearing of tweed were to pass out of fashion. A slump in tweed would have serious consequences, especially where crofting has been neglected for the loom.

THE BEAUTIES OF WESTER ROSS

THE upper reaches of Loch Carron (*above*) lie in that beautiful part of Wester Ross where Glen Carron, hemmed in between considerable mountains, broadens into a plain of pleasant pastures, bordered on the north by the highroad crossing Ross-shire from east to west, and on the south by the Dingwall–Skye railway. Quite close to the loch, and almost throughout its entire length, runs the latter to its terminus at Kyle of Lochalsh, within earshot of Skye. Without question one of the finest panoramas in Britain is that of the mountains of Kintail (*right*) seen from the steep road linking, by way of that famous mountain-pass, the Mam Ratagan, the head of Loch Duich, in Wester Ross, and the Inverness-shire parish of Glen Elg. In olden times this was the highway to Skye. It was here that Dr. Johnson's horse, "weary with the steepness of the rise" and the dead weight of its rider, faltered so much that the burly Sassenach was obliged to summon the assistance of one of the Highlanders accompanying him and Boswell to Glen Elg. Before the completion of the railway the Skye drovers, making for the Falkirk Trysts, brought their livestock this arduous way.

VILLAGES OF WESTER ROSS

KYLE OF LOCHALSH, terminus of the railway travelling westward across Ross-shire from Dingwall, was a mere hamlet consisting of a few thatched cottages until the engineers, at the beginning of the present century, blasted their way to it, thus bringing the railway to within a few feet of the tide there. Today it is the most northerly of the mainland ports from which steamers sail regularly to Skye, and to the Outer Hebrides beyond. The paddle-steamer seen in the picture above is the old *Glencoe*, familiar to those who frequent the relatively enclosed waters between Kyle and Portree. The other vessel is that which sails every afternoon (Sundays excepted) to Stornoway. Kyle is also in direct steamer communication with Harris, Benbecula, and the Uists. To the east of Kyle of Lochalsh lie those lovely sea-lochs, Alsh and Duich. A much smaller loch—Loch Long—opens north-eastwards at Dornie, the village seen in the foreground of the lower picture, where a famous Highland ferry was superseded by a splendid stone bridge just before the Second World War.

ON THE ROAD TO SKYE

ROAD and rail, bearing one another company toward Skye, emerge from the Forest of Achnashellach to part company, the former pursuing its course along the northern shore of Loch Carron, past the populous village of Jeantown (*above*) to the jetty at Strome, site of an ancient keep by the loch's narrows. At the jetty the road ends. Anyone desirous of proceeding, whether afoot or awheel, must now cross by ferry (*below*) to Stromeferry, where begins the road for Kyle of Lochalsh, and for the hamlets scattered about the shores of Alsh and Duich. The railway suffers no such interruption. Travelling along the southern shore of Loch Carron on its way to Kyle, a dozen miles ahead, it passes through its little station at Stromeferry, within a few feet of the ferrying-place and of the road leading therefrom. The crossing here can be stormy at times, especially in a south-westerly at a high flood. In misty weather, as in darkness, one summons the ferryman by clanging the bell seen in the foreground. The ingeniously designed ferry carries its load on a revolving turntable.

ON A LONELY ROAD IN SUTHERLAND

WITH less than ten inhabitants to the square mile, Sutherland is the most sparsely peopled county in Britain. Except in the case of Rogart and Lairg, which are inland parishes, its population of 13,660 is confined almost entirely to its coasts. Across its bleak interior, roads, such as that to Assynt, thread their way to hamlets by its western and north-western shores, which are indeed lonely and remote. At Skiag Bridge, that to Lochinver pursues a westward course, by Loch Assynt-side and the River Inver, while that to Unapool and the Kylesku ferry proceeds northward between the mountain masses of Glasven and Quinag. The latter road, before reaching its northern terminus by the inn at Kylesku, sends a branch off to the west, twisting and turning mile after mile, to Lochinver, by way of Drumbeg and Stoer. The picture shows a stretch of this road where it approaches Drumbeg.

THE COAST ROAD AT GRUINARD BAY

FOR coastal and cliff scenery, commend one to the wild north-west corner of Scotland, as well as to those northernmost reaches scoured by the tides of the Pentland Firth. The traveller in Wester Ross sees something of the country's primordial grandeur when journeying along the coast road skirting much of Gruinard Bay (*below*). This bay lies between Loch Ewe and Little Loch Broom. Like Loch Ewe, it has about its centre a fairly large island, now uninhabited except for sheep and seabirds. Seventy years ago, however, Gruinard Island had a population of six. The sea-cliffs of this region are matched in magnificence only by its mountains. Immediately inland from Gruinard Bay they ascend steeply to those lofty parts known as Gruinard Forest, to culminate in An Teallach, that celebrated group of ancient sandstone, on the northern cornices of which the snows lie well into the early summer.

BY LOCH DUICH

NEAR the head of lovely Loch Duich is Clachan Duich, the roofless ruin of the old church and the burying-ground of Kintail, overshadowed by the mighty mass of Ben Attow, the upper altitudes of which, in the picture above, lie shrouded in mist. Within the ruin are buried several people, most of them unchronicled. In the south wall is a tablet commemorating several chiefs of the MacRaes and their wives who were interred here. There are few roads more satisfying than the sweet-scented woodland road leading along the south shore of Loch Duich to its terminus at Totaig. By the jetty there (*left*) one hoists a rain-stained flag when wanting the ferryboat from the other side of the loch. At night one attracts attention by lighting the oil lamp kept in a box by the jetty.

CASTLES OF THE NORTH

IN 1932 the Castle of Eilean Donan (*above*), situated in Wester Ross, was opened after a restoration that had taken nearly twenty years. It has been in ruins since 1719, the year it was blown up, having been used by the Jacobites and their Spanish allies in the rising known as "The Nineteen." In 1912 the ruins were purchased by the late Colonel MacRae-Gilstrap, who now hoisted his flag upon them, claiming to be hereditary Constable of Eilean Donan in succession to his grandfather seven times removed. On a spit of land jutting out into Loch Assynt, in Sutherland, stand the ruins of Ardvreck Castle (*right*), where Montrose, a fugitive after his defeat at Carbisdale in 1650, sought refuge. Herefrom, as a prisoner, he travelled to Edinburgh and the scaffold.

THE FISHING VILLAGE OF ULLAPOOL

SITUATED on Loch Broom, thirty miles by road north-west of Garve, a station on the Dingwall–Skye railway, lies Ullapool, a village with a population of roughly six hundred, founded in 1788 by the British Fishery Society with a view to exploiting the herring-fishing industry mainly in the waters of the adjacent Minch. The industry, however, did not flourish as its founders had hoped. Consequently Ullapool was bought about 1844 by Sir James Matheson, who that year purchased also the Island of Lewis, with a view to developing both Stornoway and Ullapool as fishing ports of prime importance. Through Matheson's generosity Ullapool underwent great improvement. Though it never achieved the status planned for it, the herring industry still thrives there to a limited extent. Many of its menfolk form the crews of herring drifters; while its womenfolk are adept at gutting the fish.

DRIFTERS IN LOCH BROOM

LOCH BROOM, a sea-loch in Wester Ross, opening from the Minch at a width of more than twelve miles, continues in a south-easterly direction more than half that distance with scarcely any perceptible variation in its width. Thereafter it divides into Loch Broom proper and Little Loch Broom, the latter being much the smaller arm. The entire loch, with clusters of islands, islets, and skerries sprinkled so generously about its mouth, and with some of the ancient Torridonian sandstone mountains overshadowing it (the most remarkable of the latter, both as regards contour and colour, being Ben More Coigach), is, in the wild sense, one of the loveliest of the many fiord-like entrants of the north-west coast of Scotland. Herrings have always been plentiful in and around Loch Broom, which explains the presence in these waters of drifters such as are seen in the picture above.

FISHING INDUSTRY

THE decline of the herring fishing industry, as shown by the reports published recently by the Fishery Board for Scotland, has been one of the major concerns of those interested in that country's economic welfare. This decline has affected in no small measure the Highlands and Islands, where the number of full-time fishermen, as well as of crofter-fishermen, has fallen considerably of late. In the hope of rectifying this state of affairs, the Highlands and Islands Advisory Panel, set up in 1947, has appointed from its members a Fishery Group, whose special function is the investigation of the fishermen's problems. The picture on the left shows a number of typical West Coast fishermen such as form the crews of the herring-drifters. In the picture below one sees young women at Ullapool deftly gutting the herrings.

PEAT CUTTING IN SUTHERLAND

THROUGHOUT much of the Highlands the problem of fuel has always been an urgent one, for there are no coal-mines, and tens of thousands of acres are utterly treeless. Timber is therefore a precious commodity under such conditions. That this land once supported a rich and varied vegetation, however, is shown by its vast peat deposits. The winning of the peats, against the onset of winter, is therefore an important feature of the Highland year. The picture shows the cutting, or casting, of them in a stretch of peat-moss country.

AMONG the weirdest mountains in Britain are those of Sutherland and Wester Ross. They form part of one of the oldest and most complicated geological structures in the world, and present us with problems not wholly solved even today. This picture shows Ardmelvich Bay and the Coigach peaks, viewed in panorama from a point some miles north-west of Lochinver, in Sutherland. Cul Mor and Cul Beag (the Great Back and the Little Back) are seen roughly in the centre, at a distance of several miles. To the right of them is An Stac,

the mountain commonly known as Stack Polly. Though it attains an altitude of but 2,009 feet, it is remarkable because of its extraordinary summit, surrounded on all sides by precipitous slopes of talus and interrupted in places by shattered pinnacles of sandstone rock. The peak to the right of An Stac is Ben Eun, situated above the south shore of Loch Lurgain, which is not seen. In the left-hand side towers Suilven, better known to mountaineers and cragsmen as the Sugar Loaf. It is one of the most fantastic of all the peaks of Britain.

LOCHINVER, METROPOLIS OF ASSYNT

THE road to Assynt, in Sutherland, reaches the western sea at the trim village of Lochinver, where the River Inver, carrying its burden steeply from lovely Loch Assynt, spills noisily upon boulders covered with seawrack. The inhabitants of this village of well-built houses are employed variously. Some of them are engaged in crofting and in sea fishing. In recent years Lochinver has been increasing in popularity as the holiday resort of those disciples of Izaak Walton who find the lochs set in its mountainous hinterland a perpetual attraction. Lochinver has long been recognized as the base from which geologists and mountaineers explore the many fascinating peaks within reach of it. The peak nearest at hand is Suilven, six strenuous miles away. Its towering summit would have been seen, afar, in this picture but for the sudden descent of mist. One might describe Lochinver as the metropolis of Assynt, which includes the barren and sparsely peopled territory lying between the village and the cliffy peninsula terminating in Rhu Stoer, the most westerly point of Sutherland.

THE CLIFFS OF HANDA ISLAND

SEPARATED from the west coast of Sutherland by a channel not more than a third of a mile wide is the imposing island of Handa, consisting of sandstone in strata steeply inclined, and rising rapidly to a height of over four hundred feet, whence it falls sheer to the sea in splendid cliffs. The ledges, crannies, and fissures of these cliffs are the nesting-place of myriads of sea-birds—puffins, razorbills, fulmars, guillemots, kittiwakes, and murderous and marauding greater black-backed gulls. Handa today, except for its sea-fowl, is uninhabited. A century ago, however, it supported seven families, the ruins of whose homes may still be traced. The traditional storyteller in Sutherland still relates the exploits of a famous native of Handa—a small man known by a Gaelic patronymic showing him to have been Little John, son of Donald, son of Hugh. He was one of the MacLeods of Assynt, noted particularly for his having slain, in the days of King James VI, one of the Morrison brieves, or judges, of Lewis—a man disliked in Sutherland for his arbitrary judgments.

LOCH INCHARD AND FOINAVEN

INCHARD is typical of the many fine sea-lochs opening from the North Minch. It reaches inland a distance of five miles to Rhiconich, once an inn and fishing centre, but today merely a shooting-lodge. Its seaward parts are beset with a series of nine uninhabited islets. The mainland shores of the loch, however, are not without their crofts, such as is to be seen in the foreground of this picture, where dwellings, erected for the most part under schemes promoted by the Department of Agriculture for Scotland, have displaced almost entirely the thatched homesteads of former years. The distant mountain to the left is Foinaven, which attains, in the *Ceann Mor*, or Big Head, a height of but twenty feet short of three thousand, and is composed of white Cambrian quartzite. This gives to it the glittering aspect finding expression in its name—Foinaven, or Fionne Bheinn—the White Ben.

ISOLATED PEAKS OF SUTHERLAND

THE unusual way in which the mountain peaks of Sutherland rise suddenly out of the bleak moorland, quite isolated from one another, is well demonstrated in this picture, where we see, on the skyline, ten miles away in a southerly direction from Badcall Bay, Quinag to the right, and Beinn Leoid to the left. Quinag, the Water Spout, is certainly one of the most striking of the many masses of Torridonian sandstone rising in isolated positions at no great distance from the western seaboard of Ross and of Sutherland. Though from Inch-nadamph, on the road to Lochinver, it is easily ascended, its gullies present the cragsman with some formidable climbs. Beinn Leoid, lying between the fresh head-waters of Loch Shin and the salt waters of the fiords about Unapool, rises to an altitude of 2,597 feet, but fifty feet less than Quinag's highest point. It is by far the more isolated of the two.

HIGHLANDERS OF THE NORTH-WEST

THE crofters of the north-west coast of Scotland lead a hard and exiguous life. Such cultivated ground as exists has been wrested at great toil from moorland, rock, and swamp, over the centuries, and in face of climatic conditions which might well induce a spirit of despair and frustration. This coast is inclined to be rainy and sunless. Crops are sown late and harvested late. Winds and rains frequently delay the ingathering until well into October, by which time the corn-stooks and haystacks may be so sodden as to be of little value. Inclement weather may render impracticable access to the sea, whence the crofters derive their supplementary sustenance, fish and lobsters. Yet this remnant of a peasant population clings to its inhospitable heritage with a peculiar tenacity. It is still bilingual, speaking the Gaelic *inter se*, and a picturesque and idiomatic English when conversing with strangers.

CAPE WRATH LIGHTHOUSE

ONE of the first things the Scottish schoolboy learns is that Cape Wrath is the extreme north-westerly point of his country's mainland, that it lies beyond territory desolate and almost roadless, and that there are always three men there, manning the lighthouse known to all mariners sailing northern European waters. The lighthouse was built in 1828; and the light is normally visible for twenty-seven miles. The Norsemen of old knew well the headland upon which it stands. They called it the *Hvraf*, the turning-point. Lighthousemen are always busily engaged. When not tending the light during the hours of darkness, or the horn in time of fog, they are diligently keeping their premises spick-and-span.

THE FALLS OF ROGIE

RISING in the Derrymore hills of Ross-shire, the River Raasay (better known as the Black-water, though there are so many of the name in Scotland) flows nineteen miles to join the Conon, one of the finest of the northern rivers, famed for its salmon. A little below Loch Garve the former spills splendidly at the Falls of Rogie, amid a richness of rock and sylvan scenery prompting favourable comparison with the celebrated Falls of Tivoli, in Italy.

The Northern Highlands

THE Highlands north of Inverness, though by no means as fertile as is Moray, for example, are certainly so in comparison with the west and north-west. Roughly speaking, the lands fringing those three large inlets of the Greater Moray Firth—the Firths of Beauly, Cromarty, and Dornoch—are agricultural in the true sense. Crofting is to be found about them, of course, partly for old agrarian reasons. But, on the whole, they are devoted to large-scale farming. Here a wide margin between the hills and the eastern seaboard has been cultivated to the fullest for many generations. Where does one see grain crops heavier than in Easter Ross? Where does one find arable farming carried on more earnestly?

Between the Beauly and the Cromarty Firths lies that extensive peninsula called the Black Isle—a geographical contradiction, of course, since the sea would require to eat its way inland an additional five miles in order to insulate entirely this fertile and colourful territory. The east-coast region of Sutherland, similar in many respects to Easter Ross, is less productive, though a higher productivity per acre is resumed once we pass northward into Caithness.

The comparative fertility of this region is easily explained. A glance at a map showing its physical features immediately supplies the answer. Here the really hilly country lies farther inland. The watershed is a more extensive one. This explains the region's long and voluminous rivers. For aeons these rivers—the Beauly and the Conon, the Carron and the Oykell, the Shin and the Cassley, and so on—have been carrying eastward to the sea "the flour of the rock". Thus, great areas of such glacial and sedimentary deposit have been built up over the ages; and in places this sediment has tended to fill up such bays and corners of the firths as are not too heavily scoured by the tides. In many parts, of course, the tides have been responsible for these accumulations. The coast is therefore characterized by sandy stretches and mud-flats. We see this at the head of the Cromarty Firth. We see it again in the Ardroy Sands and in the Nigg Sands. We see it even more conspicuously in the case of the Dornoch Firth. A considerable area of mud-flats, such as the Dutch might well have recovered, lies exposed at its head during ebb water, while at its seaward end, on both sides, great stretches of alluvium render navigation impracticable. On the north we have the Cuthill and the Dornoch Sands: on the south the Edderton and the Whiteness.

A little farther north we see, in Loch Fleet, another excellent example of marine silting. The nature of the shore, as well as that of the waters lying offshore, and within the territorial limit, explains how white fishing, rather than herring fishing, has long been pursued, industriously and profitably, by its littoral inhabitants. Several communities, such as Embo and Portmahomack, have derived their livelihood almost solely from the sea. Indeed, the line-fishing of the entire Moray Firth has been a rich and agreeable inheritance from earliest times, though these are the waters from which, every now and again, come protests against trawlers operating within prohibited areas, thus ruining the more prolific fishing-banks.

The climate of this region is very different from that on the west coast in the same latitude. The latter is apt to be rainy. Temperatures there are generally higher, and are less liable to extremes. Snow lies for no length of time, except on the loftier peaks. In short, the climate is more maritime. On the east, however, the rainfall is more moderate, and sunshine more usual. Indeed, certain areas of the Moray Firth are noted for the number of hours during which the sun shines brightly and warmly—a very important factor in agriculture. Whereas the meagre crops in the north and north-west often never ripen, even in the late autumn, owing to the winds and rains, here they do so early, drooping in heaviness, waiting for the harvesters to garner them.

On the other hand, if this region have less rain and more sun in summer, it has more snow or more prolonged cold in winter. Its climate is harsher and drier. Indeed, it is inclined to be of the continental, rather than of the maritime, type. The snell east winds of the North Sea give the air a sharpness rather than a touch of drowsiness. Snow falls abundantly and lies long. All this has an important effect upon rural economy. Snow is a great conserver of heat. Fields that have lain long under it deliver, in due season, a rich harvest.

The great glory of these particular parts is their rivers. Consider with them that fascinating waterway, the Kyle of Sutherland, and one sees how admirably they are watered by nature. Though the rivers have their cataracts, such as the Falls of Shin and the Falls of Rogie, they are very different from their short and impetuous neighbours draining the *western* watershed. Their salmon-fishings are famous. So are their duck-shootings, though I can never understand why anyone should want to bring down anything so beautiful in flight as a wild duck or goose.

The *genius loci*, by the way, is no longer Prince Charlie, but Montrose. The countryfolk are well versed in the Marquis's triumphs and ordeals. They readily point out the scenes associated with him in the north—the clump of trees at Ardgay, for instance, where General Strachan's forces encamped the night before engaging him in defeat at Carbisdale, a few miles away. They call it Strachan's Wood. They know, too, the battlefield of Carbisdale itself, and the tiny pond at Culrain (said to be bottomless!) into which Montrose and his followers are believed to have flung arms and jewels after their rout; and they point to the spots where, in flight from the stricken field, they essayed to cross the Kyle of Sutherland.

FEARN ABBEY, EASTER ROSS

IN 1221 Ferchar MacTaggart, Earl of Ross, founded in the Easter Ross parish of Fearn
the Premonstratensian Abbey of Fearn. The fifteenth of its abbots was Patrick Hamilton
(1503–28), the protomartyr of the Reformation in Scotland, burnt at the stake at St.
Andrews. From the Dissolution until 1742 it served as the parish church. On a Sunday in
October of the latter year, its ponderous roof collapsed, killing forty-four worshippers.
The Abbey lay in ruins till 1772, when it was repaired to serve anew as the parish church.

MILL OF KINCARDINE

In Easter Ross, a region known for its excellent husbandry, old mills driven by water-wheels, such as that at Kincardine (*above*), were common. In recent decades these mills have largely fallen into desuetude, their ponderous wheels having rusted to complete immobility, their millponds and lades filled with the silt of generations and overgrown with rank vegetation.

SEAT OF THE CHISHOLM

Near the left bank of the Beauly River there stands, in a fine park surrounded by wooded hills, the modernized Erchless Castle (*left*), lofty and narrow. Since the fifteenth century it has been the seat of The Chisholm, chief of this once powerful clan. The Chisholms were fervent Jacobites; and those of the name are proud of the fact that the definite article precedes the name of but three personages—the King, the Pope, and The Chisholm!

112

NORTH KESSOCK VILLAGE AND BEAULY FIRTH

BETWEEN the shires of Inverness and Ross, on the east coast, intervene the Inner Moray Firth (sometimes termed the Inverness Firth) and the Beauly Firth, the latter being the inner extension of the former. Between South Kessock, on the Inverness side, and North Kessock, on the Ross, plies the well-known Kessock Ferry. South Kessock is but a couple of miles due north of the town of Inverness. Across the strait lies that fertile part of the Ross-shire mainland known as the Black Isle. Our picture shows the ferry-steamer at its pier on the Inverness side of the strait. On the opposite shore is seen the village of North Kessock, backed by fertile fields distributed here and there upon a hillside steep and densely timbered. The westward view from mid-channel, toward the head of the Beauly Firth, is one of the finest in a region as luscious as it is lovely. Ferrying has gone on here from time immemorial.

ARDGAY PANORAMA

IF THE south-easterly prospect of the picture above have points of beauty and of interest, no less so has the north-westerly prospect (*right*) from Cnocnamoine, the Hill of the Peats, situated at Ardgay, within calling distance of the Jubilee Hill, and described very fully in the author's book, *The Goat-Wife: Portrait of a Village*. At the right-hand side of our picture is seen the innermost reach of the Dornoch Firth, close to which runs the highroad to the Far North. This road is carried across the Kyle of Sutherland at Bonar-Bridge, seen in the background beyond the point at which the road seems to disappear. Here the Kyle is narrowest: here Kyle begins and Firth ends. The foreground is part of Easter Ross: the background is Sutherland. Between the two, and at the base of the distant range of hills, the long, narrow Kyle runs inland for some miles to the estuary waters of the Rivers Shin and Oykell. In the middle-distance, barely visible, yet another river—the Carron—flows broadly into the Kyle.

DORNOCH FIRTH

THOUGH the head of the Dornoch Firth is in no sense remote, it is unquestionably one of the loveliest localities on the east coast. The inner arm of the firth (*left*), viewed in a south-easterly direction from the Jubilee Hill, behind the village of Ardgay, in Ross-shire, would appear to be enclosed completely by the distant rampart of mountains reaching its climax in the Struie Hill —the summit about the centre of the picture. Immediately to the left of this hill may be seen the Doune of Creich. Between the Doune and Struie occurs the channel to the outer part of the firth. At the base of the Struie range, and quite close to the shore, run road and railway. Through the dip in the skyline in the right-hand corner travels the old drove-road between the Far North and the southern cattle and sheep markets. It passes over the moors by way of that secluded hostelry, the Aultnamain Inn, bringing one down to within a few hundred yards of the Cromarty Firth, a mile or two beyond Alness. In pre-railway days, when Ardgay was noted for its ancient annual fair, drovers and cattle dealers making for it were obliged to bring their livestock by Aultnamain, since there existed no other road.

THE RIVER CARRON

THE River Carron receives its waters from a number of small tributaries draining the mountains and glens in the Ross-shire parish of Kincardine, west of Amat. Therefrom it flows eastward through Strath Carron to enter the Kyle of Sutherland opposite Bonar-Bridge. Hugh Miller, who as a lad visited it in 1820, describes in *My Schools and Schoolmasters* "the dark hills and alder-skirted river of Strath Carron". This river has been the scene of spates and floods which at times have swept devastatingly over the farmlands at Invercharron, near its mouth. On the mantelpiece of a house at Ardgay is a jar containing fish carried into the garden at Invercharron House by the great flood of September, 1908.

116

DORNOCH

THE Meikle Ferry is to the Dornoch Firth what the Kessock Ferry is to the Beauly. It enables one to pass between Ross and Sutherland without having to travel circuitously round the head of the firth at Ardgay and Bonar-Bridge. Our picture on the right shows a cyclist on the Ross-shire side hailing the ferryman from the Sutherland. In 1812 the ferryboat broke in two and nearly a hundred of its occupants were drowned. By the northern shore of the Dornoch Firth stands Dornoch, county town of Sutherland, an ancient and royal burgh. Possessing two golf-courses (one of which is seen below), it is one of Scotland's most celebrated golfing centres. Dornoch Cathedral (its spire is seen in the picture) is among the finest ecclesiastical buildings in the north. At Dornoch in 1722 took place the last execution in Scotland for witchcraft.

TAIN AND CROMARTY

BY THE southern shore of the Dornoch
Firth, almost opposite the town of
Dornoch, stands Tain, a royal and
municipal burgh known in olden
times by a Gaelic name signifying its
associations with a famous saint. St.
Duthus is said to have been born in
the year 1000, at the site of St.
Duthus's Chapel. He died at Armagh
in 1065. Nearly two hundred years
later his body was "translated" for
burial at Tain. The ruined chapel
bearing his name is believed to mark
the spot "quhair he wes borne".
This spot was once a famous garth or
sanctuary. To it, in 1306, there fled
Isabella, Queen of Robert the Bruce,
his daughter Marjory, a number of
ladies-in-waiting, and some attendant
knights. The fugitives, who had fled
from Kildrummy Castle, were seized
in St. Duthus's Chapel by the Earl of
Ross, who handed them over to
Edward I. The ladies were im-
prisoned: the knights were executed.
Adjoining the court-house, and now
forming its imposing entrance, is an
ancient, square tower (*top, left*), once
a prison. It contains the town clock,
and a sweet-toned bell founded in
Holland in 1616. Only a few miles
south of Tain, upon a flat promontory
on the southern shore of the narrow
entrance to the Cromarty Firth, is
Cromarty itself, a little town with a
population of about eight hundred.
For centuries the older part of the
town has been the residence of fisher-
folk. Here, in times more industrious,
the making of sailcloth was a thriving
occupation. Cromarty is proud of its
most celebrated native, Hugh Miller
(1802–56), who began life as a stone-
mason and became renowned as a
geologist, author, and thinker. His
thatched birthplace (*bottom, left*), is
now a museum housing his relics.

HELMSDALE

STANDING at the mouth of the River Helmsdale, in the parish of Kildonan, is the coastal village of Helmsdale, long an important centre of the fishing industry. Helmsdale's harbour is one of the best on the east coast of Sutherland, which explains largely how it has remained for years the headquarters of the fishing district stretching from Embo to Dunbeath. On the right bank of the river, a little below Helmsdale's bridge, are the ruins of a castle built in 1488 by the seventh Countess of Sutherland as a hunting-seat, and noted as the scene, in July, 1567, of the murder of the eleventh Earl and his Countess. They were both poisoned at supper by the Earl's aunt, Isabel, who would also have poisoned their son had not her own son drunk by mistake the fatal cup she had mixed. Her son died two days later. Five days later the Earl and Countess were dead. The wretched poisoner committed suicide at Edinburgh on the day appointed for her execution. George, fourth Earl of Caithness, was said to have instigated her in those nefarious designs of which she was later found guilty.

INTO the Kyle of Sutherland fall three rivers of no mean size, each well known to the angler—the Carron, the Oykell, and the Shin. Memories of these carry the writer back to the early years of the present century, back to the days of jolty brakes and picnic-baskets. Transport by means of internal combustion had scarcely penetrated as far north then, owing largely to the unsuitability of the northern roads. At that time a journey from Ardgay or Bonar-Bridge to Lairg, following northward the course of the Shin from its mouth at Invershin to its source at the southern end of Loch Shin, had to be undertaken by pony and trap, if not by cart or on foot. Bicycles were still uncommon in these undulating parts. True, the Highland Railway Company would have conveyed one to Lairg station, located at least a

THE RIVER SHIN

couple of miles from the village of the same name. But those who fished the Shin went by road rather than by rail. Today they travel these parts swiftly by car. In those times an expedition to the Falls of Shin (*left*) took on something of the quality of Paradise itself. Here one watched the salmon running upstream—leaping clear of the tumbling, rumbling waters in heroic attempts which fascinated. The Shin is a river of no great length. From source to mouth it is less than eight miles. Yet its entire course is picturesque. Much of it is well wooded. A mile or so north of its mouth is Inveran, where the road to Lairg is carried across it by the bridge seen in the picture above. At this point, too, diverts to the westward the road to Assynt, by way of Strath Oykell and the vast moorland beyond.

SALMON FISHERS' BOTHY

THE salmon fishings of Ross and of Sutherland have greatly increased in value in recent years—those of the Kyle of Sutherland especially so. The picture (*left*) shows a corner of the Kyle at Bonar-Bridge. In the distance stands the salmon fishers' bothy. Nearer at hand their nets are hanging.

LOCH GARVE

WITHIN a mile of Garve station, on the Dingwall–Skye railway, is Loch Garve (*below*), one of the many lovely freshwater lakes lying deep in the mountainous country on every hand. Its shores are well wooded; and the abundance of heather and of wild flowers in its vicinity explains the beehives seen close to the cottage.

THE KYLE OF SUTHERLAND

THE Kyle of Sutherland is surely one of the glories of the Northern Highlands. Properly speaking, it comprises the inland reaches of such of the Dornoch Firth's tidal waters as have penetrated far inland between Ross and Sutherland. It commences at Bonar-Bridge, and for the first mile or two it runs northwards, narrowly confined, to be amplified by the River Carron. Then it broadens out into that exquisite lake known as the Maikle Pool, narrowing again thereafter as it approaches Balblair. This picture shows a stretch of the Kyle seen from the woody crags behind the fertile fields of Balblair farm, in Sutherland, with the twin peaks of Carn Bhren, in Ross, on the horizon. Northward it insinuates thereafter, ever narrowing until it passes beyond the old ferrying-place at Invershin. It now widens again below Carbisdale, and then sends its tidal overflow far up Strath Oykell.

CARBISDALE CASTLE

EARLY in the present century there was built at Culrain, in Ross, for the Dowager Duchess of Sutherland, that splendidly situated edifice, Carbisdale Castle, overlooking the Kyle of Sutherland, perched like some fantastic Rhineland stronghold of Wagnerian opera. The building boasts a sturdy clock-tower, and has some excellent work in stone and in wood. The panelling of the dining-room is a commendable piece of workmanship. A few years ago the Castle was presented to the Scottish Youth Hostels Association. An old man, whom the writer knew, heard pipes playing under what, today, is the Castle's rocky site. What an unseen piper was doing there, he could not imagine, though he felt sure these unaccountable strains foretold great changes in the locality. Shortly afterwards men arrived on the scene to blast out a firm foundation for the Castle. Close by is the plain where, in 1650, at the Battle of Carbisdale, the Great Marquis suffered defeat at the hands of General Strachan.

SKIBO CASTLE

"THE castles and pyles of Southerland at Dornogh, Dunrobin (the Erle of Southerland his speciall residence) . . . Skibo, wher ther is a fair orchard in quhilk ther be excellent cherries." Thus wrote Sir Robert Gordon in 1630. No part of the Skibo Castle of his day remains. Its place has been taken by the massive successor erected by Andrew Carnegie (1839–1919), and depicted above. Skibo Castle was the Scottish residence of this remarkable man whose beneficence to Scotland seems almost to have been forgotten. The Castle occupies a unique position near the head of an inlet of the Dornoch Firth, four miles west of the town of Dornoch. The scenes from its lofty towers are truly magnificent. It was to an earlier Skibo Castle that Montrose, after Carbisdale, was brought captive from Assynt. Therefrom he was conducted to Tain, and then to Brahan, and finally to execution at Edinburgh. At Skibo he was given the seat of honour—a mark of deference quickly denounced by General Strachan.

SCOTLAND'S NORTHERNMOST COAST

EASTWARD from Cape Wrath to the border of Caithness, the northern coast of Sutherland presents a spectacle of wild and desolate beauty. Several sea-lochs penetrate it, such as Loch Eriboll, the Kyle of Durness, and the Kyle of Tongue. Though it is true that roads of a somewhat secondary character now reach most of the isolated townships scattered about this northern coast, much of it remains unfrequented except by the more curious and adventurous. The scenery is unique where the sandstone cliffs are lofty and formidable. Never a tree is to be seen. Yet their absence is not regretted. On the contrary, their presence would seem incongruous. The colourings of sward and sand, of red cliff and black skerry, of sea-pools green and blue and purple, of wild flowers that, like the catmint and the red clover, lend a warming glow to a land windswept and drenched in the spume of the northern seas, are all the traveller asks for. Roads, like that seen in the picture (*above*), will beckon him irresistibly to such crofting townships as Durness. There, if he be geologically minded, he will find ample to engage his attention. A mile to the east of Durness he will come upon the Cave of Smoo, into which he may wander a distance of four hundred and fifty feet. The mouth of this monstrous cavern is a hundred and ten feet wide and fifty-three high. It attracts to these shores many interested in Nature's more unusual manifestations.

INDEX TO PHOTOGRAPHS

ACKNOWLEDGEMENTS

The photographs in this book were taken by the author, with the exception of those supplied by the following and appearing on the pages indicated: British Railways (Scottish Region), 68 (*centre*); J. Allan Cash, 60, 76, 84, 87, 92, 96, 97, 98 (*top*), 99, 103, 104, 105, 106, 107, 127; The Forestry Commission, 80, 81; Ian G. Gilchrist, 63; Brodrick Haldane, 7, 20 (*bottom, right*), 31, 34, 39, 44; David Innes, 35, 38, 61, 98 (*bottom*); H. D. Keilor, 93, 119, 126; A. D. S. Macpherson, 13, 100–1; North of Scotland Hydro-electric Board, 64, 66; The Scottish Tourist Board, 2; E. W. Tattersall, 4, 10; Topical Press, 65, 67, 71. The publishers wish to thank all the above for permission to reproduce copyright material.